Puppy Training Made Easy

Mick Gordon

Copyright © 2019 by Mick Gordon

All rights reserved. No part of this book may be used or reproduced by any means, graphic, electronic, or mechanical, including photocopying, recording, taping, or by any information storage retrieval system, without the written permission of the publisher except in the case of brief quotations embodied in critical articles and reviews.

Contents

Introduction 1

Chapter 1: 11 Tips on Choosing a New Dog-friend 4

Finances 4

Puppy or Fully Grown? 5

Development 6

Gender 7

Time Factor 8

Safety at Home 8

Pecking Order 8

Equipment 9

What's in a name? 9

Chapter 2: Which Breed is Best for You? 11

What to look for in a Reputable Breeder? 12

Beagle 19

Bulldog 20

Collie 22

Golden Retriever 24

Labrador 25

Pug 26

Wheaten Terrier 26

Summary 27

Chapter 3: What's Going on in a Puppy's Mind? 30

What's a puppy thinking now that he's lost his familiar smells and sounds?...................30

Settling-in Period 30

Is Your Puppy Happy? 33

Separation Anxiety................................36

Sleeping Arrangements..........................38

A Puppy's Behavior...............................40

Chapter 4: Relationship between you and Puppy 44

How do I make the puppy my friend?.................45

Trust...45

Verbal Communication 45

Body Language......................................47

Puppy Play 48

Quality Time 50

9 Scientific Reasons: Why your Puppy Will Increase your own Health Benefits 54

Chapter 5: Toilet Training 59

Early Training 59

Routine 60

Signs that Puppy Needs the Toilet 62

Chapter 6: To use a Crate or not? 66

A crate is not a prison. 66

Pros 68

Cons 70

Alternatives 72

Dog Technology 73

Chapter 7: Basic Behavior Training in the Home 75

Basic Training Commands 76

Tips on Training the Puppy 77

Be Consistent 77

Patience 78

Time 78

Biting 79

Treats 80

Look 80

Sit 81

Stay 82

Come 83

Leash 84

Barking 85

Chapter 8: Vaccinations and Puppy Academy 88

Puppy's Vaccinations 89

6-8 weeks old 89

10-12 weeks old 89

12-24 weeks old 90

14-16 weeks old 91

1-1.5 years old 91

2 years old 91

Pet Insurance 93

Puppy School 97

Equipment 100

Finding a Puppy Trainer 101

Chapter 9: Socializing 106

Dog Descendants 106

Instincts 108

The More the Merrier 108

Integration of New Friends 109

Chapter 10: How to Choose the Right Food ... 113

Balanced Goodness 113

    Energy compounds 114

    Proteins 114

    Fats 114

    Minerals 115

Overfeeding 115

Symptoms of GDV: 116

Feeding Schedule 117

Types of Food 118

Homemade 118

Tinned Foods 122

Kibble or Dry Foods 122

Toxic Foods for Dogs 123

Chapter 11: Grooming 125

Dog's Coat 125

Hair Coat 126

Fur Coat 126

Shedding 127

Puppy Coat 128

Bathing 128

Grooming Services 129

Chapter 12: Traveling 133

Safety Travel for Dogs 134

Type of Vehicle 134

Securing your Dog 135

Training Puppy to Travel 137

6 Travel Tips for Dogs 139

Leaving Puppy Behind 142

Boarding Kennels 142

Private Sitter 144

Chapter 13: The Dreaded Worms and Fleas 145

Internal Parasites 145

Hookworms 146

Roundworms 146

Tapeworms 147

Whipworms 148

Heart-worms 149

Fleas 149

Home Remedy for Infestation of Fleas 150

Preventative Treatment Against Fleas 153

Chapter 14: Possible Health Care Problems..... 154

Common Illness 156

Diarrhea 156

Sickness 156

Common Diseases in Puppies 158

Parvovirus 158

Distemper 159

Kennel Cough 159

Skin Irritation..160

Other Health Issues 161

Neutering..161

Self-Inflicted..162

Old Age 163

Life Span..165

Conclusion... 167

Introduction

Congratulations – you've made the life-changing decision to include a dog as part of your family.

Yet, a dog is more than just a pet. You have chosen to have a very special friend in your life because a dog is many things including:

- ❖ A loyal friend who will stay by your side for years to come.
- ❖ A companion who will show you unlimited and unconditional affection.
- ❖ A complex character full of feelings and emotions.

These are only a few of the reasons why a dog is man's best friend.

How then do you decide from the hundreds of breeds that exist, which dog is best for your family? Where do you start?

This guide sets out factors that will ensure your puppy lives a long and happy life. First, consider the 11 tips on choosing your new friend. Chances are you've already thought through each of these ideas already. That's because they are such important issues on making a happy home for your puppy. With these points in mind, you can move on to consider some of the more popular breeds. Our guide will give you an idea of typical character traits.

Once your puppy is home, it's time to begin the basic stages of training. A dog needs basic discipline to help him feel secure. Some new owners pamper their pooches without realizing the consequences. This can lead to bad and uncontrollable behavior. For instance, some owners feed a dog under the table as you eat. Then they wonder why their dog begs for food at the table and may even punish the dog. This gives off conflicting messages, and the dog would often become confused. He's unable to understand what is expected of him.

The true nature of a dog means that he has enough intelligence to abide by your rules as long as he knows them. It's much better to be firm and consistent. Let your puppy understand the difference between good and bad behavior. Lay down those permanent rules, such as not jumping on the furniture, right from the start. You should NEVER physically punish a dog for any reason whatsoever. It is cruel and unnecessary.

In the 1800s, social reformer Jeremy Bentham wrote about animals, "It is not whether they can reason or talk but whether they suffer."

Along with the awareness of animal welfare, our love for dogs as family friends has increased substantially. Your puppy needs love, and he needs to learn his new home is a safe place. Nothing more complicated than that.

A dog will soon become your companion and friend, no matter how you treat him. That is how loyal a dog can be. To return that friendship and affection, you will be rewarded tenfold. Let him know his boundaries, and he will be content. He will reward you with a lifetime of loyalty and devotion. There is nothing more satisfying than having a true friend in your life.

Chapter 1

11 Tips on Choosing a New Dog-friend

There are a few things to think about before you make the decision to bring a dog into your life. Let's have a look at eleven important factors that you need to be considering. By looking closer at each of these points, you will have a better idea of the changes that are about to take place in your life.

Finances

1. First, you should look at your finances. It's better to determine if you can actually afford to keep an extra family member. In America, the ASPCA (American Society for the Prevention of Cruelty to Animals) has recently calculated the average cost, in the first year, of keeping a dog. This will run at around $1,800. The good news is that after the first year, it drops to

around $500 a year. Ask yourself how you feel about these figures?

2. Our second point is also in relation to a financial aspect. Can you afford medical insurance? The average annual dog insurance can run at around $400. Bear in mind that this won't include regular boosters, and it might even have a cap to how much you can claim. Now then, you might think that this figure seems a bit steep. Actually, it's an insignificant number when you consider how much an illness or accident might cost if you don't have insurance. Full kidney treatment can be around $2000. Even worse, if you couldn't afford the bill at the time, your only other option will be euthanasia, which really should be the last resort. Shop around for the best dog insurance that suits your needs. It's well worth it.

Puppy or Fully Grown?

3. At number three, I want to mention that although we're discussing puppies in this guide, you might prefer to get a fully-grown dog.

Raising a puppy can be very satisfying, but it's not the right solution for everyone. If you decide to get a fully- grown adult dog, you should still read this guide. Your new dog-friend might need a little re-training to make sure it's happy in its new home.

Development

4. The fourth factor you need to consider is how big your puppy is going to grow to. This is important in relation to your environment. For example, it's a bad idea to have a large dog in a small apartment. Big dogs need room to move around. Otherwise, they will feel miserable. You might even find your home becoming filled with the aroma of your dog if it's big in proportion to space. In this same category, think about the size of your backyard, or maybe, you don't even have one. If your puppy doesn't have access to a garden area, then get one that won't outgrow your space.
5. Number five is similar to my last point, but this is more in relation to deciding on the breed of

dog you want. Consider not only size but also the temperament of the breed. Will it be good with kids? How active is it going to be? What type of coat will it have when it's fully grown? A dog with thick curly hair will need grooming often. Even a dog with short hair will shed hairs on your furniture. It doesn't hurt to think about the problems you might come across as your puppy begins to mature.

Gender

6. In sixth place is the need to consider the sex of your prospective puppy. If you don't want more puppies running around, then you really should have your dog neutered, whatever the sex. A neutered dog is generally better behaved, particularly males. If you have an un-neutered female, there's nothing worse than walking a dog around that's on the heat. It will attract all the male dogs, and it will be a frightening experience for both you and your beloved pet.

Time Factor

7. Okay, we're almost done, but in seventh place, I want you to consider how much exercise you are able to give your dog? For example, if you're out at work all day and the dog's left alone, then it's going to get bored stuck at home. A situation like that is very unfair to the dog because it can lead to bad behaviors, such as chewing through the furniture.

Safety at Home

8. Number eight is to consider the safety aspect of your backyard. Is it fenced off so your dog can't escape?. Dogs are very resourceful. If there's a way out, they will find it.

Pecking Order

9. Number nine is to ask you if you have the right approach to be a firm dog owner? Every dog, even the timid ones, need a basic amount of training to keep them safe. You'll need to be strict with your dog in certain circumstances.

Don't allow it to bark all day long and teach it good toilet training habits. A dog feels safe when you set boundaries for it. This is all about the pecking order, and you need to be right at the top.

Equipment

10. Finally, our last and tenth point is to make sure you buy all the right equipment you're going to need. Consider if you want to cage-train? If so, it's important to introduce them to their cage right from the start. Don't forget all the things a dog needs to help it settle in. A puppy or a younger dog needs toys to wear down that energy. A dog wants to go for walks, so don't forget the lead and harness, food bowls and grooming brushes, doggy bags, and doggy trays. The list is long, so have everything ready before your puppy arrives.

What's in a name?

11. Once you have the puppy home, start by using his name when you talk to him, so he becomes

familiar with it. When deciding upon his name, try to find one with at least two syllables. That's because he's going to be learning one-syllable words such as "no" and "stay" quite a lot over the next few months. So choose a name that he can differentiate from the one-word commands. Of course, if he's a pedigree, he may already have a name, but do shorten his name if it's long.

You want your puppy to have a loving and safe home. Better that you're well prepared and you've sorted out any obvious problems beforehand. Everyone loves a puppy, but to do it right, there are a few basic rules to learn. This guide will cover everything you need to know so that your puppy has a happy, safe home.

Chapter 2

WHICH BREED IS BEST FOR YOU?

We've looked at some of the issues to consider when making the decision to bring a puppy into your family home. How then do you decide which breed is best for your family?

For much of the decision, it's a case of following your gut instincts. They say that when we buy a home, we know within seconds of walking through the door if we're going to be happy there. Of course, you can't compare an inanimate house with a living dog, but there is still some truth to this maxim. Because all puppies are so cute, the chances are that you will fall in love with the whole litter immediately. That's why it's best to make those important decisions before you see them.

If you're buying from a breeder, you may not even get to choose which puppy is yours from the litter. That is unless you've left instructions with the breeder early on in the process. Breed and temperament are factors you can decide upon beforehand. To help you make that decision, you need to consider some basic influencing aspects, such as:

- ❖ Have you got children?
- ❖ Do you have other pets?
- ❖ What size dog is best for the size of your home?
- ❖ How much time you have with regard to walking and exercise?
- ❖ Does the prospect of dog hairs around your home bother you?

These are but a few scenarios to think about. Before we go on to assessing a few of the various breeds, let's consider what to look for in the breeder who is selling puppies:

What to look for in a Reputable Breeder?

Once you've made that all-important decision that you can welcome a puppy into your home, the next step is to find a breeder. So, where do you begin?

You can contact the Kennel Club Association (KCA) for your country. In the US, this would be the American Kennel Club (AKC). They can provide you with a list of variously- approved breeders. They also allow advertising of available puppies. Be careful though because any breeder, recognized or not, can advertise on the AKC website.

There are also the breeding clubs, each one specific to a particular breed. Local vets will be a good first port of call as they will be familiar with the more respected and trusted breeders. Do plenty of research for reviews of the breeder that you choose.

You should also SERIOUSLY consider taking in a shelter puppy if you can. They often have pedigrees if you want a specific breed. Sadly, they have an abundance of unloved dogs, including puppies. A puppy from a shelter is well-cared for once in the shelter. You can rest assured that he has passed many health checks and got all his shots. He is ready to find a forever home.

A caring breeder will not continually produce litters of puppies. They love their dogs and don't use them as a production line. Most will only breed each dog once a year. The mother (bitch) will only produce around four litters throughout her lifespan. Further, the mother should be over a year old, so her body is matured enough. Because they care, they will show good knowledge about the breed that they raise. They may even have records of competitions they have won with their dogs.

Here's an important to-do list, once you've made contact with your breeder:

- ❖ Visit the breeder and ask to see the parent dogs or at least the mother. Assess her temperament as this will give you an idea if this breed is for you or not. Note how content she is in her own home. Is she nervy or friendly? Does she look healthy? Is her environment clean?
- ❖ Ask the breeder questions and also expect them to ask you questions too. A good breeder will want their puppies to go to good homes. Ask if you can come and visit the puppy before taking

it home. You want to see how content it is with its litter and be assured it has had a good start in life.

- ❖ Note the surroundings where the dogs are kept. Are they clean and comfortable?
- ❖ Do not accept a puppy under 8-weeks old. It is not ready to leave the litter, and neither is the mother ready to be separated from it.
- ❖ A good breeder that cares about the pups may ask you to sign a clause to say you will return the puppy if things don't work out. They only want to make sure their puppies are happy; it is not an insult to you and your family. Even with the best of intentions, the relationship may not work out for a multitude of reasons.
- ❖ Top breeders often have waiting lists, so that's a good indicator that they have a good reputation.
- ❖ You will get a health clearance certificate for your puppy. You may also be provided with genealogy papers if you buy a pedigree that is club-registered. Plus, you will also get a bill of sale.

AVOID puppy-mills or backyard breeders. These unscrupulous breeders are only concerned about profit. Puppy-mills do not care about the health of the parents or the puppies. Even worse, the chances are their prices will be lower to lure you in, but don't be fooled. The puppy-mill will breed many different dogs.

The backyard breeder may only breed their own pets to make a little extra cash. This in itself is not problematic, so long as they do it correctly. You are not likely to have any official documents such as kennel club registration or health records. Moreover, there will be no genetic screening to ensure the breed doesn't carry through any health problems. Your pet will not be neutered and may even have an illness due to lack of care.

What to look out for in a disreputable breeder:

- ❖ It is unlikely that you will be allowed to visit the parent dogs if it is a puppy mill.
- ❖ If you can visit, look out for bad smells and unclean areas. This can only cause health problems for young pups. If you suspect foul

play, DO report them to the local animal welfare groups, even if only anonymously.

- ❖ You will not be offered a certificate of health or any other official documents.
- ❖ The person selling you the puppy will have little knowledge of a specific breed.
- ❖ They will have a constant supply of puppies, not only because they have many adult dogs, but also because they breed their dogs throughout the year. They do not adhere to the once a year guideline, so the mother may well be exhausted.
- ❖ They will most likely allow you to take the dog before he turns 8 weeks. Possibly, they may not inform you of the correct age to get around this problem.
- ❖ They will offer to meet up with you for the transaction of your puppy. You may never see the site where they are born.
- ❖ The puppy may shy away from you because it has had no sympathetic human handling. Look out for health issues such as runny eyes, dry

nose, unkempt coat, skin irritations, and a general lack of energy.

They may get around many of these pitfalls, so trust your own instincts. If you feel something is not quite right in the process of purchasing your puppy, don't go ahead. You may end up with a sick dog, and you won't be doing the other dogs in the puppy mill any favors. It might be distressing, but if they aren't making money, they will find another avenue to follow.

A good breeder cares about the puppies because they love the parent(s) and want to find the best homes possible. If you don't get that vibe, then simply walk away. It will be hard. Again, we reiterate that if you have serious concerns about the breeder and the dogs they are selling, you can report them. Contact an animal welfare charity, such as the ASPCA. They are very discreet because at the end of the day they only want what is best for the animals concerned.

Now it's time to look at some of the more popular breeds and see how each one might fit into certain situations.

Beagle

If you have young children, you might prefer a smaller puppy that won't knock over the kids in its excitement.

A Beagle puppy will be as inquisitive as the kids. They are clever pups that will engage with the children in a calm manner. Originally bred to hunt, this is a puppy that will love to be outdoors playing in the backyard.

It gets on well with other dogs because they are bred as pack dogs. It's probably not a good breed for you if you don't have a backyard though. It does need plenty of exercise throughout its development. On the other hand, that's a great excuse to get its humans out to the park.

It can withstand living outdoors so long as it has a warm shelter and bed. If you want to do this, bear in mind that it's not a breed that likes to be alone. Its fur is short but thick so it may shed hairs a little. Whilst it doesn't require much grooming, it's still a good idea to brush the coat about once a week to tackle any loose hairs. Plus, grooming is a time to bond, so get the kids helping out.

Bulldog

This is a noble dog that represents spirit and determination. Because of breeding traits, it's not one of the most energetic of dogs. Bulldogs make lovable and loyal companions. There are a few distinct separate types that fall under the Bulldog category.

English Bulldog

It is medium in height and stocky in the body with short legs. They have a short stubby snout and folds of wrinkled skin on their faces, with sagging jowls. They're not everyone's idea of an attractive dog but don't let that put you off. They make great family pets and get on well with children as well as other pets in the same household. As well as a gentle nature, Bulldogs have a reputation for courage. It's probably a throwback to their origins of being bred for bull baiting. This small but chunky dog will take well to a small apartment as he likes a relaxed lifestyle.

They have typical flat features that can lead to problems with breathing. This causes their breathing to sound labored after exercise. Those wrinkles to the facial skin will need attention from time to time to avoid skin infections. As with most short-haired dogs, their coat needs only a minimum of maintenance. A good brush down once a week should do it. This not only deals with loose hairs but will feel good on his skin.

Olde English Bulldog

This is a more recent American breed of bulldog. It is also known as the Leavitt Bulldog, named after the breeder. It was developed in the 1970s in an attempt to create a healthier type of bulldog. Their appearance is more athletic, and they don't suffer from as many health problems as the traditional English Bulldog.

French Bulldog

These are smaller than the traditional bulldog breed. They are a mix between the English Bulldog and French rat-catching Terrier. Proving popular with city life, they make great small apartment companions. They do need rather a lot of maintenance though. It is a breed that still suffers from a limited breathing issue. They also struggle to control their body temperature and must wear a coat when it's cold. In hot weather, they may need air conditioning so they can cope with the heat. Many airlines refuse to carry French Bulldogs because of such issues. Their coat and nails will need regular attention. This is a breed that can suffer bad separation anxiety, so it should not be left alone for long periods of time. Being a quiet breed they can be a little shy. They do make a great family pet, and despite their small size, they love to protect members of the family, most especially the females.

Collie

There are many different types of collie breeds, and they're classed as a medium-large dog. You can also get long and short-haired varieties. They have an excellent temperament, making them a great family pet, most especially for an active family. Their intelligence makes them easier to train, and they're not mischievous by nature. Because they are clever dogs, they can become bored when left unattended for too long.

Originally bred for herding, they can be a little on the possessive side with family members. If they show signs of attempting to herd the kids in at the park, you need to discourage such behavior straight away.

The two most common types of Collie are:

Rough Collie

This is the classic Lassie-type dog that we all know and love from the movies. It was bred in Scotland, UK, for herding. It is classed as a medium to large-sized dog. They're usually long haired with a sable (golden brown with black tips) and white coloring although the darkness of the browns can vary. It's a breed that is excellent around children and sociable with other animals. They have a double-layered coat that will need regular grooming.

Border Collie

This is another Collie. It originated from Scotland and was bred for herding sheep. It's a highly intelligent and very athletic breed. They require lots of activity to keep them occupied with regular and extended exercises. Otherwise, they will suffer boredom, and we all know that a bored dog is a mischievous dog. They are not suitable for apartment living. The Border is smaller than the Rough Collie and classed as a medium-sized dog. Whilst usually black and white in color, they can also come in mottled colors. Peppery grey is not unusual, or there can even be patches of brown in their coats. Border Collies have a double coat that sheds and needs regular grooming.

Golden Retriever

It's a medium or large-sized intelligent breed, quick to learn and easy to train. It's a popular dog with families because they have a great temperament. They have a golden coat of various shades and were originally bred to retrieve game birds, hence the name. They love to bounce around with their long legs and wag their long-haired tails anywhere and everywhere. They may need supervising when among young children as they can jump and become giddy. Not that they would harm them intentionally, but they can be a heavy dog, up to 35kg for a male.

The shed their coat heavily and will need regular grooming.

Labrador

It's a breed with high intelligence and lovable nature. It is also known as the Labrador Retriever as they too were originally bred to retrieve game. Although it's a similar-sized dog to the Golden Retriever, this one usually has a short coat. Training should be easy as these are another intelligent breed. They mix with other pets quite well. He can grow into a large, stocky dog, and you will have to watch his weight as he grows older. It's not a good breed for a small apartment. He needs room to run around, or he might become overweight and clumsy.

He loves to play and need lots of exercises, so having a backyard is a must. He's short-coated so should only need that weekly brush down. Labradors feel completely at home in the water, even very cold water, as their dense coats are waterproof. It's their favorite pastime to splash around and also to retrieve the ball or stick you've thrown.

Pug

It's a small dog originally bred in China. It's often known as a Royal Dog as it was a favorite of emperors and royalty when first introduced in Europe. Its size makes it ideal for the smaller home. The short snout can cause breathing problems which can lead to difficulties regulating temperature. Another problem is that their bulging eyes are prone to damage. You would be well advised to take out full comprehensive pet insurance for this breed. Like many dogs, he likes his food, so watch his weight. He has a short coat, so will not shed hairs too often.

Despite its small size, it is quite an energetic little mutt. They enjoy adult companionship but will also happily play with the kids.

Wheaten Terrier

I've mentioned this relatively obscure dog because it's classed as hypoallergenic. Whilst no dog can be completely hypoallergenic to everyone, the soft coat reduces the risk for some sufferers. Its coat is actually hair, so they shed only a few hairs daily. Because it is hair, it will need trimming at regular intervals and brushing to avoid matting.

It is a small or medium-sized dog. Males can reach up to 20kg in weight. Soft Coated Wheaten Terriers are friendly and playful dogs and get along with children and other pets. This makes them an ideal family pet.

Summary

This book could not possibly cover all the varying breeds of dogs. The Fédération Cynologique Internationale FCI), is an association of the international Kennel Clubs. They recognize 344 different breeds in total. I've tried to list some of the more popular breeds, but there are many more to choose from. One important point to make is that you should not be put off by the reasons they were first bred such as the bull terrier type dogs were sadly bred to fight. The American Pit-bull has a fearsome reputation and is often categorized as a fighting dog. Yet, they are also known as a Nanny dog because they are so good with children. Most Bull Terrier breeds have wonderful natures and make ideal family pets.

Working dogs make great pets too, but they will have boundless energy. The German Shepherd, or Alsatian, was first bred to be a working dog. These intelligent breeds can still make great family pets. What you may find is that they don't take well to strangers. Such dogs can become possessive of their family. Because they are clever by nature, they need to be kept occupied or will become bored all too quickly. This will then lead to behavioral problems.

Avoid over guarding by using good training techniques, which we'll discuss later in this book. Any dog that shows a strong, aggressive character will need to have solid training from a young age. Intelligent dogs can be highly strung. But you can ease this problem for them with good training skills. Once they've mastered your requirements, they are ideal companions.

When considering the various breeds, take into account how much exercise and grooming they'll need. Larger breeds often need a special diet for stronger bones and joints. We'll discuss food in another chapter. Giant breeds should not be over exercised until they're almost 2 years old and their bones have matured. Toy breeds can have a variety of inbred health problems. Low blood sugar (Hypoglycemia) causes them to shake and quiver, which can be distressing. Long-haired breeds, as you would expect, need a regular grooming routine. It's sensible to consider all the known factors of the different breeds of dogs.

Most of all, look at the temperament of the breed, especially if you have children. As we showed with the Pit Bull Terrier, it has a fearsome reputation, but in reality, this breed has a very soft nature. Your puppy is coming to live with you at a very young age, so you can train him to adapt to your family needs.

Chapter 3

What's Going on in a Puppy's Mind?

What's a puppy thinking now that he's lost his familiar smells and sounds?

Settling-in Period

There's enough scientific evidence to show that dogs feel the basic emotions of fear, love, and even jealousy. Such emotions are controlled through hormonal release, much the same as for humans. Their reasonably-high intelligence has given them a good understanding of human body language. Having evolved around us for thousands of years, dogs have become our close domesticated companions.

Note that I mentioned "basic" emotions. That's because many people believe dogs understand every emotion their owners feel. Contrary to popular belief, there's no scientific evidence to prove this. A dog does not experience cognitive thoughts such as pride, shame, or even grief. For example:

An adult dog who's lost its owner through death can settle with a new owner quite easily so long as the dog is shown affection and doesn't experience fear.

If you find your dog red-handed rummaging around in the bin, you might think he has a guilty look on his face. What he's learned is that he's about to be punished, even if it's just the tone of your voice. What you see on his face is the anticipation of a reprimand.

The sound of a calm, encouraging voice fussing over them is very comforting for a dog. These may even be new types of experiences for your puppy. So far, he's been mostly in the company of his mother and siblings. This new sort of human attention will help him to feel safe.

Your puppy has been taken away from his comfort zone and is now in a strange environment. It's up to you, as their new carer, to make sure they acclimatize to their new surroundings. Be patient. They will need time to learn all the new, unfamiliar smells. There are a few steps you can take though, that will help them settle in as quickly as possible:

- ❖ The first point is with regard to their little whimpers. The chances are it's because they feel anxious, especially at night time. You can help ease that anxiety by comforting them, speaking to them in a calm, light tone. Stroke them gently as this will help too. Don't get cross with them, even when your eyes refuse to stay open. They will sense any negative emotion in your voice, which will make them even more anxious.

- ❖ Secondly, you need to organize beforehand how you're going to toilet them during the night. Perhaps, it can be a litter tray or a trip outside to the backyard. With a bit of luck, they may have had some basic house-training, but if not, be patient when they have accidents. If you are persistent, they will soon understand what they need to be doing.

- ❖ The last point is to ensure that Puppy feels safe. When you put him back in his bed, give him a soft blanket and a teddy to replace the feel of his litter-mates.

Puppies seek attention because they need social interaction. This is innate in all breeds of dog as they are pack animals. The puppy will thrive on affection. He will appear happy when he knows you've noticed him with lots of fuss. This will become important when you are absent and then return. Don't ignore the puppy when you return. Calmly acknowledge how glad you are to see him, just as much as he is to see you.

Is Your Puppy Happy?

It's okay to spoil the puppy a little in his first week. Once he's become familiar with his new smells, it's time to stop jumping to his every need. Otherwise, he may become demanding. Even at this young age, your puppy needs to know his place in the pack, which is now within your family. If you have children, teach them to be firm with him, so he knows that he is lower in the pecking order than they are. This sounds harsh, but dogs rely on a pecking order. This is what makes them feel safe and secure. Like most social creatures, he needs rules and routine. They are two very important factors for his happiness. What other signs can you look out for to make sure the puppy is not miserable?

We all know a tail wag can mean a happy dog. However, no matter how much you might want it to be true, that wide-mouthed grin isn't a smile. What is true though is that dogs do have a range of facial expressions. Changing expressions not only exhibit their internal feelings, but they are also communicating with us. One study suggests that when humans look at them, dogs can use a number of facial expressions in return. They may show their tongue or lift their eyebrows to make their eyes larger, a trait many humans find cute. One interesting result of this study is that dogs more likely to do these movements when humans are facing them.

- ❖ Dogs of all types enjoy affection, such as a stroke or gentle pat. But dogs are not necessarily comfortable if you try to hug them. Some may even physically pull away or growl a warning because this is not a natural behavior for them.

- We know that a wagging tail can mean they are happy to see us, but they can read our facial expressions too. They will use certain movements in our face to determine our reaction to them. As subtle as it may seem, a rise of an eyebrow can indicate affection to the dog.
- If the puppy brushes up to your legs or leans onto you when sitting next to you, it's a sign of trust. Another classic sign of trust is if your puppy lays his head on your lap.
- As your dog learns to trust you, it will become more confident with eye contact. Eye contact is often seen as a challenge for dogs, so don't stare in the eyes of a dog you are not familiar with.
- Dogs can even copy their owners when they yawn. This is quite a remarkable behavior as it seems to show that they empathize with us. Empathy was believed to be a trait of only a few animals, such as primates. Yet, studies are suggesting that dogs can indeed show empathy. It's still early to conclude anything, and more research still needs to be done to prove this to be true.

Separation Anxiety

When the puppy first arrives at his new home, remember he doesn't know who you are. The puppy may become anxious at the separation from his mom and siblings.

Ideally, puppies will stay with their litter and mother until they are at least eight weeks old. If they're too young, they'll miss out on that all-important gradual weaning stage. Pups are much like mammals in that they need all the goodness of their mother's milk.

There are a few problems that can be attributed to taking pups from their mom too early.

A major one is that they might not gain enough weight. If they don't, it can lead to a weak immune system and result in a sickly puppy.

A study conducted in 2011 showed that puppies who weaned too early could have a few behavioral problems, such as:

- ❖ Excessive barking.
- ❖ Separation anxiety.

- ❖ Destructiveness.
- ❖ Fearful of loud noises.
- ❖ Possessiveness.
- ❖ Tail chasing.

Early weaning can be problematic both for the dog and its new owner, who will have to contend with such issues. Given this, isn't it then essential to buy a puppy from a respected and registered breeder? The breeder should be one that you know actually cares about the mom and her litter.

Even then, a good dealer can't guarantee that your puppy isn't going to miss its mom and siblings. So far in its life, they have been everything it has ever known. The closeness of its litter-mates and mom were its entire world. When sleeping, they would have bedded down in close contact with each other, which fosters a feeling of safety. Now, all that has gone, the puppy has no maternal comfort.

To ease this transition, you could give the puppy a bit of natural medicinal help, with ADAPTIL Junior. It's a natural product used for calming dogs. It's made up of pheromones that the puppy would have smelled from the mother's mammary glands. You can buy the product as a collar or a spray, and it's odorless to humans although its success is dependent on how much other support the puppy will have. You, as the carer, still need to show your puppy affection, so it will lead to him feeling secure.

Sleeping Arrangements

This is an age-old problem for owners of new puppies. Should they sleep alone or with you? Sleeping alone in a strange home will be a very scary experience for a puppy. If you have other dogs, you could try putting your puppy with them, but make sure he's introduced to them under supervision before you leave him alone with them. Most adult dogs will not harm a puppy, but you want all your dogs to feel comfortable with the newest member, so consider the older dog's emotions too.

It might be better though if the first week is spent in human company. As the puppy adapts to its new home and family, you can gradually move its bed to the room he'll spend more time in. After a week in your bedroom, try moving his bed outside your door, leaving the door open. Over the next few weeks, move his bed further away from your bedroom door. When you feel confident he's not going to fret, put his bed in his permanent room. His bed is his little private haven. Once he's familiar with it, he'll feel safe in there.

If you don't want your new puppy to sleep in your bedroom, then at least provide it with a soft and warm bed of his own. You could use a hot water bottle with a soft fluffy cover. There are even soft toys called "Smart Pets" that you can buy. They heat up and make heart beating sounds. It might help to substitute the warmth and closeness of its mom and litter-mates. If you are getting a Puppy from a good breeder, ask them for help in the transition. See if you can place a small toy or blanket into the bed he shares with his litter before you take him home. The smell of his mom and siblings will remain on the toy and offer some comfort in their new, strange home.

If your intention is to use a dog crate, you need to start with this immediately. The puppy can become accustomed to it from the onset. Make up a bed for him in the crate, and for the first week, situate it in your bedroom.

Whatever you decide, be prepared for a restless night. Your new puppy will cry, and you will need to get up to toilet them.

With a good breeder, he must have already had a good start in life, learning much from his mother and siblings. For instance, through play with litter-mates, he would have learned that teeth could hurt. The breeder should have started the weaning, so he will no longer need milk and be chewing on solid food. His socializing may even have extended beyond his litter-mates. The breeder may have introduced other dogs and people. All these life lessons are essential for a puppy to learn about the world around him.

A Puppy's Behavior

Some animal psychologists and vets believe that there are specific periods in a dog's life when their behavior can be shaped. It could be due to brain development or survival instincts from when dogs were in the wild. No one yet understands why they might be more susceptible at these particular ages.

- ❖ The first important phase of development is when the puppy is 8-12 weeks. This is the time he joins you, so it's important to understand how to care for him when you take him home.
- ❖ The second period is around 4-9 months old. He's still a puppy, but he is settled with his new family.
- ❖ The final stage is around 1-1½ years old.

As his new carer, you should become familiar with your dog's body language, just as he is learning to understand yours. If he begins to hide at loud noises or his ears go back and his tail goes down between his legs, he's showing signs of fear. Don't allow this to continue. Find out what he's fearful of and slowly introduce him to it. Is it a delivery at the door? Is it a stranger coming into his home or a sudden loud noise? With your help, any new experience that he feels afraid of can soon be dealt with. Encourage him to face whatever it is he fears, so he learns that it will not harm him.

There are many ways he reads messages from you, so it's important you get it right. Let's have a look at some examples of how you might affect his growing behavior:

- ❖ Don't be angry or shout at the puppy because it's whining. If you yell at him, he will sense your anger, and you'll lose his trust in you. He needs comfort, not fear.
- ❖ Do the usual checklist of providing comfort, such as checking if he's hungry or if he needs toileting.
- ❖ If he continues to whine and you're confident nothing is wrong, then you must learn to ignore him. Place his crate or bed in another room, so you can have some time out. Turn on the radio at a low volume, so he has a little background noise. It's important that you don't allow your own emotions to overcome you because he's relying on you to make sure he feels safe.

For instance, let's say you're in the kitchen trying to get the dinner ready. If he whines for attention, put his bed or crate in the room with you, and talk to him or even sing from a distance. The sound of your voice may be all he needs.

One bit of good news is that puppies need around 18-20 hours of sleep a day. No matter how demanding they may be, sooner or later, you will get that well-deserved rest. The bad news though is that he may not sleep through the night until he's around 4 months old. That's why you need to take them to the toilet before he goes to bed and during the night. It may be a few months before he does not need to go to the toilet at night time.

All in all, if you train your puppy with a loving approach, then you will gain his respect. The puppy will become loyal to all those he considers belong in his pack. That bond will be very, very special for him and for you too.

Chapter 4

Relationship between you and Puppy

Mutual respect is an important element of any relationship, and that goes for dogs too. I've discussed how dogs feel similar basic emotions as humans. It stands to reason then that if you show them respect, they will return that respect tenfold. When I talk about respect, I'm referring to treating your dog with compassion and care.

I also brushed on the topic in chapter one, of teaching your children to be firm with your puppy as it grows. Dogs live naturally with a hierarchal status in their pack. By knowing its place in the pack, you're helping the puppy to have a sense of belonging. Being part of a group makes him feel safe.

Whilst you don't need to have a dog from the stage he is a puppy, to build up a mutually respectful relationship from puppyhood does give you an advantage. He'll soon forget the home he came from, and all he will know from then onwards is his new family. In his mind, his family is his pack.

How do I make the puppy my friend?

Trust

Trust is number one on this list. Just as with any new friend, you will need to build up trust between you. When he's making whimpering noises at night because he's lonely, he's going to remember the smell of the person or people who come and make him feel better. You are going to be seeing to all his needs when he leaves his mother, which is the first point of your new bond. In effect, you have become the leader of his pack.

Verbal Communication

This is the second important factor in building a relationship between you your puppy. Stay calm when you speak to him. It's not always about the words you say, but the tone of your voice too. For example, shouting at a child for every minor misbehavior could cause that child to fear you. It's much the same for a puppy. There is also growing evidence that your dog may actually understand some of the words you use.

A study published in Current Biology used brain scans to determine how dogs process speech in humans. The results showed that they treat speech in much the same way as we do. The left hemisphere of the brain processes the vocabulary. The right hemisphere processes the emotion in words by the tone. They claim that a dog is not fooled by using positive praise out of context. For example, if you replace the words, "good boy," with "happy days," the dog will not be fooled, not even if you are using a positive tone. Brain scans showed that in such cases, the left side of the brain that processes the vocabulary was not activated. Hence, the dogs were not fooled by the trickery of words alone.

Okay, your puppy isn't going to get a degree in languages anytime soon. He is, however, going to grow up and learn what certain words mean. For instance, if a grown dog has its name changed, at first, it will not respond to the new word. After repetitive training, it will start to understand the new word and its meaning.

Only then will the dog begin to respond to its new name.

Who's a clever doggy then!

Body Language

This is the third important factor. You must learn what messages he's giving you through his body movements. Humans use their hands to express non-verbal communication whereas dogs use their tails. They also use their tongue, ears, eyes, and stance. Plus, they vocalize with barking, whimpering, or even howling.

A puppy's body isn't going to know how to use a wide range of body language. He can't communicate this way yet because he hasn't learned much about it. A puppy shows basic emotions when moving his body, such as wagging his tail when happy or licking you to show affection. If he's afraid, his ears and tail might go down, and his eyes may look away from you. He may even try to hide. As he matures, he will begin using more intricate movements, such as pacing at the door for the toilet. You too must learn doggy-speak by recognizing his body language and the noises he makes.

A chilled dog is easy to spot as his body will feel loose as opposed to twitching with tense muscles. He may even open his mouth and pant a little. He will not mind eye to eye contact with the people he knows, with wagging tail and relaxed ears or laying on his back for a tummy rub. If he's attacking you with tongue licks because he loves you, he's releasing endorphins that will reduce stress.

However, if he's anxious, his panting will become faster. His eyes may open wide, and he won't blink much. It's unlikely he'll make eye contact with you. The muscles on his body will become tense, so you can tell he's uptight. Because he's panting fast, he may also drool. Often, dogs who are anxious will shed bits of fur from their coats. If he's afraid of a more dominant dog in his presence, he may raise his hackles. He's readying for a fight or flight response.

Puppy Play

For number four, let's talk about puppy play. He would have been practicing social play with his siblings since about 3-weeks old. It's difficult to predict his temperament at such a young age. That's because puppies play by being both dominant and submissive whilst learning. He would have learned how to yap, wrestle, and chase, with his litter-mates. Chances are he'll leap around one minute and run away the next, and such actions are all quite normal.

Play though is important in building up your relationship together. You have now replaced his litter-mates. To begin with, you could use a large soft toy that he can associate with a sibling. Shake it around, and he'll yap, play-nip, pull, pin it down, or even mount it. Everything's a game to him. This is the stage where you are going to build up his confidence, so you need to do it right. His interactions with you will form a life-long attachment.

We've talked about communications, but we all know there's more to a relationship than just that. Spending time with your new dog can lift your mood as well as the dog's.

Quality Time

Our fifth topic focuses on quality time with your new best doggie friend (BFF).

Puppy is not going to be able to go out of the backyard until he is around 12 weeks old due to vaccinations. This means he has to get his exercise in the home. He has lots of energy, so how are you going to wear him out? A puppy needs around 15 minutes a day of walking time, for every month in his age. He's coming to you at around 2 months old, so you need to spend at least half-an-hour running him around. It doesn't need to be in one session, but consider that energetic half-hour as his basic exercise time.

For each month, add another 5 minutes to his walk-time. By the age of 3 months when he can go out to public places, you'll need to be walking him for at least 45 minutes. By the time he's an adult dog, he may need more than one walk a day to tire him out in a natural, healthy way.

Time spent with the puppy is not only about exercise. It is an opportune moment to focus on giving him your undivided attention. If you're going to get a puppy, then consider it as a dependent. Your puppy needs affection, attention, and education too. We've talked about how you need to learn dog-talk and how the play is a must for any youngster.

Massaging a puppy will not only provide that all-important quality time together, but it will help to build a trusting bond. By giving your puppy a regular 10-minute massage, you are making it easy to see to his other needs throughout his life. Grooming will be easier because he will get used to the close contact. As he gets older, you will be able to relieve his aching joints should he get arthritis. It's all about the puppy learning to trust the close contact and you giving your dog a little basic maintenance. What you will learn is:

- ❖ How warm he normally feels so you can notice any changes in body temperature.
- ❖ Where swellings might begin to appear as he grows, so you can keep an eye on them.
- ❖ If he gets any dry skin.

- ❖ How tense his body feels. If he becomes ill, when you touch certain areas, he may indicate they are painful.

By massaging him from puppyhood, you are learning about his body so you can be his carer throughout his life. Plus, he will learn to enjoy his massage.

So, how are you going to begin this relaxing process for him? Well, here's a few tips on getting started:

- ❖ All dogs love a tummy rub, so that's your first point of contact. With the palm of your hand, gently rub over his chest and belly.
- ❖ He can stay on his back, but make your way towards his neck muscles. Knead any muscles a little between thumb and forefinger.
- ❖ Work your way around his body where his main muscles are, such as rubbing the top of each leg.
- ❖ Give him a little rub in places he can't reach, such as the pits of his legs and the back of his ears.

- ❖ Wrap your hand around the bottom of his legs and press gently. Work your way from his paws to the top of the leg.
- ❖ Check between his toes, gently rubbing each one to see if there are any seeds or splinters present.
- ❖ Encourage him to get up, so you can stroke his back, and anywhere else you couldn't reach. It helps to stimulate nerves as you move his skin around.

This will only take around 10 minutes once you're used to doing it as a part of his quality-time routine.

If you were to add all the time together devoted to your puppy's needs throughout the day, it wouldn't come to much more than a couple of hours. That's why it's important to make it quality time spent together.

One good way to keep him by your side, whichever room of the house you're working in, is to consider crate-training. That way, he can sit in his crate while you're busy, and he can still see you. When you're not so busy, let him out to run around. If he's with you around the home, then he won't get lonely. He doesn't need your attention all the time to bond with you. But, he needs to know you're there for him wherever he is.

The worst thing you can do is invite a puppy into your home and then leave it alone all day while everyone in the family is out. Relationships take trust and time. He cannot possibly trust someone is not there and doesn't spend time with him. Even if you hire a dog-sitter to let him out, that's no compensation for quality time spent with his family.

9 Scientific Reasons: Why your Puppy Will Increase your own Health Benefits

One of the obvious health benefits of owning a dog is the increase in exercise. There are other benefits that will also improve your general health and wellbeing.

1. Because you will get at least a 30-minute walk a day, you're improving the health of your heart. As well as strengthening muscles all over your body, you will be getting more vitamin D from the sunlight, even when it isn't sunny!

You could walk more and lose weight if you wanted to include that into your daily doggy routine too.

2. It is scientifically proven that stroking your dog can lower your heart rate and therefore your blood pressure. It can also lower your stress levels because a dog lowers the cortisol hormone levels you produce, which, again, is good for your heart. Instead, you actually produce more dopamine which is a feel-good hormone.

3. As your grubby dog is busy spreading bacteria, he is helping to make you more immune to certain diseases.

4. Growing up with dog hairs flying around the home helps children to overcome certain allergies. Their immune system is exposed to everything a dog's coat can throw at them, so they build up resistance. One study outlined in the Micro-Biomed Center (BMC) 2017 shows that children raised with a dog had an abundance of certain bacteria that helped fight allergies, such as asthma and eczema.

5. Another research study outlined in the PLOS One journal 2015 shows that people who have companion pets, such as dogs, are likely to be more sociable. Social isolation has been acknowledged as a general risk factor for poor health, so owning a dog could be the answer. Walking your dog can be very much a social activity. You could find that you chat with other strangers who are also walking their dogs. This often happens simply because the two dogs bump into each other and begin their sniffing routine. In this study, 40% of owners admitted getting to know others in their neighborhood by owning a pet.
6. Other studies have shown that an "only" child does better with self-esteem if they have a dog as a family pet. They are more likely to join in activities and be less withdrawn.
7. Owning a dog reveals something about your own personality too. Studies have shown that people who own dogs tend to be more outgoing than people who do not. Of course, it may be because outgoing people are more likely to own

dogs. There is also research that shows a correlation between what type of dog you choose and your own personality. That's because certain types of personality are drawn to certain breeds.

8. People who own dogs live longer than people who do not, states a 12-year-long study of over 3-million people done by Upsalla University in 2017. The results could not prove the causal effect, only that there was a link between lifespan and dog ownership or non-ownership. Whether it's because dog owners are more active, can fight off bacteria better, or have lower stress levels, is not clear. Most likely, it is the combination of all these effects.

9. Dogs don't only improve your physical health but also your mental health too. They make perfect companions for single people or for those suffering grief from a loss or even those who are healing from ill health. One study proved this by allowing dogs to visit the residents in an elderly facility. The residents showed vast improvements in their mental

capability during the period when the dogs visited. Kawamura and colleagues (2007)

Taking on a puppy means devoting time to get to know his character. Allowing time for him to get to know his new environment is safe. If you're giving him a happy home, then set some time aside to be with him. A dog feels loneliness in much the same way as a human does. Enjoy every moment you can together because you are about to have a very special and unique friendship.

Chapter 5

Toilet Training

One of the first things you will want to teach your puppy will be toilet training. Otherwise, your home is going to have a rather distinct, unpleasant smell.

Early Training

Before you go to bed, the puppy should visit the backyard for a 10-minute session. Stay with him, so if he relieves himself, you can praise him. Find a command word that he will begin to associate with relieving himself and being praised for it. Phrases such as, "wee-wee," "potty time," or even "toilet," but use the same phrase for this task every time.

If he manages to do what's expected of him and in the right place, the praise is important. You're letting him know what a good boy he is and how he'll get attention when he behaves himself. It means keeping a close eye on him all the time. His pees will be tiny and quick, so you might miss them if you're not on your guard.

If you don't have a backyard, this is a good time to introduce your puppy to a special dog-training tray. These are specially-made trays. You can use disposable, absorbent pads in them if you wish. In the first few weeks, the tray will need to follow him around wherever you put his bed. Once he's settled in his new home, situate the tray in its permanent place. If you are using it indoors but still have an outdoor area, gradually move the tray towards the outer door. It's not a good idea to move it around too much, or he'll get confused. It is all trial and error I'm afraid. Despite all the precautions you take, there will no doubt be accidents. Puppies are not textbooks, but they will understand if you keep up their training.

Routine

You must build up a good routine for his toileting needs.

Get yourself into the habit of taking your puppy either outside or to the designated area indoors on a regular basis. Here are the timings that you can fix to help build up your routine:

- First thing in the morning when you get up.
- Before meals and around 15 minutes after every meal.
- Last thing at night before he's going to his bed.
- Plus, every 2 hours as puppies don't have much control over their bladders.

Other factors that will help his toileting routine are:

- Making sure he's fed at regular intervals, such as similar times every day.
- Check you're giving him the right amount of food, so you don't overfeed.
- Take away the water bowl about an hour before his last toileting at night time.
- It's a good idea to have him on his leash for his toilet session outside. Lead him to the area that you want him to use for a toilet.
- Don't abandon him out in the yard on his own. Stay with him when you let him out in the yard or on the tray. Once he's done his toileting, praise him with some petting.
- NEVER yell at him or rub his nose in his waste if he has an accident. This will only scare him

and make him fear you. If he does have an accident, then ignore him while you clean it up. He'll soon realize he's done it wrong when no praise comes his way.

- ❖ Wash indoor accidents up thoroughly with ammonia-free detergents. His sense of smell will lead him back to the same spot and encourage him to go there again if you don't.

Signs that Puppy Needs the Toilet

Hopefully, you're building up a great routine to encourage the puppy to get with the program. Even so, it will still be difficult in those first few months. In-between the routine, you also need to watch him for signs that he's about to go to the toilet in a place where he shouldn't. Here are a few signs to watch out for in his behavior:

- ❖ He might start to do a frantic circle while he sniffs at the ground.
- ❖ Then there's the obvious squatting his back end down. Male puppies will wee in the same position as females at that age. They haven't yet

learned to balance with a leg up. That will happen between 6 months and 1 year of age. The actual reason for raising a leg whilst urinating is to leave his scent, so it's instinctual.

- ❖ Is he whining? Don't forget the basic checklist that includes, "Does he need the toilet?"
- ❖ As he matures, he may begin to pace by the door. That's a great sign that he's getting the hang of doing it outdoors.
- ❖ If he's already had a toilet accident, he may attempt to go back to that same spot because he can still smell it. Watch out for this little trick and give the spot another clean with an ammonia-free product. It might smell clean to you, but remember a dog's sense of smell is far greater than a human's.

Your puppy will not have accidents intentionally. His body is not yet developed enough to always be able to wait for his routine cue. As you get to know his abilities, you can adjust your routine according to how he takes to it. Some dogs are more intelligent than others and will pick up on your signals within a few weeks. Others may take months to get the message.

Whatever you do, don't chastise him for an accident. If anything, simply ignore the puppy and clean up the mess. If you catch him in time before he has the accident, here are a few tips:

- ❖ Carry him to his allocated area.
- ❖ When you put him down, give him your chosen command word.
- ❖ If he runs off and doesn't attempt to do anything, pick him up a few times and bring him back to repeat the process.
- ❖ Should he still not have done anything, leave it half an hour, but keep your eye on him.
- ❖ Try the process again.
- ❖ When he finally does it in the right place, don't forget the praise and treat.

The main rules when toilet training are:

- ❖ Routine.
- ❖ Praise with and without treats.
- ❖ Ignore accidents.

- Use non-ammonia detergents for cleaning accidents.
- Patience and kindness.

Chapter 6

To use a Crate or not?

A crate is not a prison.

Whether to use a crate or not for your new puppy can be a somewhat difficult decision for any new dog owner. The thought of any living creature confined within bars invokes a sense of loss of being a prisoner. Yet, to a dog who's trained correctly, this can become a place of safety. There are positives and negatives for using a crate to train your dog. The decision, in the end, is up to you. Let's have a look at this topic in more detail to help you see what your options are.

From the first night of owning your new puppy, a crate is a useful place to put him while he settles down at night. All he needs is a soft, comfortable bed inside the crate. It's up to you whether you leave the door open or shut. At least, if it's shut, it means he can't get out and wander off. If you decide to shut it, you might want to put down some newspapers for his accidents. The chances are the cage will seem large to him, if you've bought it based on his expected grown-up size. At least, there should be plenty of room in there to start with. If you keep the crate door open, then he may sneak out and have accidents on the carpets, so do be prepared.

Don't allow him to pee in the crate for longer than the first week. Grown dogs don't like to mess where they sleep, so begin his toilet routine as soon as you can. For the first week, it acts as a "means to an end" to help the puppy get used to his new environment.

The size of a crate should be large enough to allow a full-grown dog to be able to turn around and stand up. But, for a puppy, we can put that aside as he's going to grow into it. Alternatively, you could buy a smaller crate and replace it as he's growing. This is the better option, but it can become costly.

Puppy needs to feel that his crate is a safe, secure place to sleep in. For you, it is a mobile enclosure. It means you can place the crate in whichever room you are busy working in. He's out of harm's way, and he can also see you. That's a win-win situation. There's no reason why he can't have toys and treats in his crate. However, you might not want to put a water bowl in there as it might end up in a puddle on the crate floor.

What then are the pros and cons with regard to crate training?

Pros

- ❖ It's not a prison. Leave the door open most of the time, so the puppy can come and go as he pleases. Shut the door at training times only or when you need to keep him in one place for safety reasons.
- ❖ The crate is his and his alone. Of course, you need to clean it out, and he needs to accept that you might have to go in there on the odd occasion. Remember though that even dogs need their own space sometimes.
- ❖ It can be the place where he sleeps if you place his bed in there. Once he's trained, you can leave the door open for him to come and go as he pleases.
- ❖ It's a great place to throw his toys inside when he's not playing with them, helping to keep your home tidy.

- ❖ If he must be left alone for any length of time, it will keep him safe and stop him from doing any damage to your home.
- ❖ As a guide, at 8-10-weeks old, your puppy can stay in his crate for up to an hour. For every month he grows, you can increase this by another hour. An adult dog can be left in a crate for up to 8 hours, but it's not recommended to do that too often.
- ❖ You can train him to go in his crate when visitors call particularly if he's barking at the door. He can always come out later, so they can meet him.
- ❖ Having your dog crate-trained helps with toilet training and reduces destructive behavior.
- ❖ Pad the floor of the crate once you're sure he's toilet trained, even if it's only with blankets. It needs to be a warm and comfortable place.
- ❖ It's a great way to stop the puppy from begging at the table at meal times by placing him in his crate out of the way while you eat.
- ❖ Finally, crates are useful for traveling; they keep your dog safe in a vehicle.

Cons

- ❖ Dogs are not den-creatures in the wild unless they are ill or have a litter. It seems then a little cruel to some that they are forced into a confined space for any length of time.

- ❖ Some consider putting an animal in a crate for long periods of time to be cruel. It would be cruel if done for many hours at a time. Dogs throughout the world are crate trained and mostly very happy and content pets. The recommendations for an adult dog is no longer than 8 hours. That seems an awfully long time to be locked away in a small space and all alone. If you work all day, try and get a dog walker to split the time up a little.

- ❖ It is true that some dogs can become distressed in a crate, but that's all dependent on the dog's temperament. If your puppy shows lots of distress when going in a crate, re-assess how important the crate training really is.

- A dog kept locked in a crate for long hours will become bored. This could have a detrimental effect on their general mental health.
- The wrong-sized crate can indeed harm the dog's growth. An adult dog should be able to turn around and stand up in a crate, so his joints and muscles are free to move. It should be the same for a puppy but starting with a smaller crate. If he's in a large crate, he will most likely go to the toilet in there too. The problem with this though is that you will need to keep buying bigger crates as your puppy grows.
- Should a dog go to the toilet in the crate, it will be stuck in its own mess until the owner arrives home.
- On a hot day, a dog in a crate may not get enough ventilation if not put in an aerated place. Equally, in colder months, it doesn't want to be in a draft.
- If a dog is crated whilst wearing a collar, it might get caught on the bars and be unable to

breathe. This is dangerous if no one is around to help.

Alternatives

As you can see, there are plenty of good and bad reasons for crate training. However, there are alternative methods for keeping your dog safe when you can't always be around:

- ❖ Fit baby gates to the doorways of his regular room. So long as the room is dog-proofed, the puppy can run around and stay safe. You can also place his bed and his toilet tray in the same room at opposite ends. This is much better than in a confined space.
- ❖ Keep your puppy in a dog-pen, much the same as keeping a baby in a baby-pen. This is a small area fenced off with pen walls. They don't tend to have a roof, so make sure the puppy cannot jump over the fence. Often, the fencing is partitioned and folds away when not in use. You can then tidy it away when not needed.

- ❖ Outdoor kennels are also an option if you don't want your dog in the house. This can be a good recourse for larger breeds. Such kennels should be waterproof and have a roof. You could even provide a heated bed mat or put heating in there if there's an electrical hook up. Of course, do look at the safety aspect of fitting electrical heaters into an outdoor kennel area.
- ❖ Hire someone to come in and exercise your puppy while you are out of the house. It is good company for them too, rather than being on their own for long periods at a time.

Dog Technology

There are other ways to keep your eye on your puppy while you're away. There's a way whereby you can even talk to him and give him treats in your absence. You can do all this with the help of technology.

- ❖ It's all done with a camera, which is ideal if you have the puppy in a safe dog-proofed room while you're away. Through software applications, you can interact with your puppy from your phone or smartwatch. Watch him and speak to him when he looks a bit down in the dumps. Nothing will cheer him up more than to hear your voice though he can't see you. He might even come up to the camera looking for you. As he sniffs his wet nose around looking for you, it's a great moment to snap a picture. Most of these specially-designed cameras are remotely controlled to swivel and tilt. That means you can survey the whole room.

- ❖ Some models are also treat-dispensers, which you fill up before you leave the house. When he comes up to the camera, you can pop out a treat from the specially-positioned hole. If you want to keep your eye on the puppy at night time, many also have night vision.

I haven't yet mentioned how well a crate can help with training. Let's move on and look at some of the basic house training methods and also see how a crate can help with them.

Chapter 7

BASIC BEHAVIOR TRAINING IN THE HOME

For the puppy's safety and wellbeing, you must begin training as soon as possible, most especially the basic behavior commands that will help him fit into his new environment. Such a young dog is only going to have a short attention span, so don't expect great things in the early days. Chances are he's already recognizing his name and coming to you when you call him. Training is good for mental stimulation which all youngsters need. Don't skip out the training sessions and then expect the puppy to behave himself. At this stage, it's more about helping him to adjust to the world, so he's going to be a happy dog.

If you want him to do competitive sports training, that shouldn't begin until he's around 6 months old. For now, though, it's only about some basic discipline, so he can fit in better with his new family.

As with human children, young dogs will test how much they can get away with, not that they do this on purpose. Both children and puppies are curious and adventurous creatures. But, when you have a mouthful of sharp teeth, the last thing you want is to let him go around nipping people with them. Some ground rules are required. Otherwise, he may grow up to be a mischievous nuisance. You want to enjoy your time together, and that won't happen if he doesn't understand social behavior.

Basic Training Commands

Besides his basic toilet training, as discussed in chapter 5, there are other basic behaviors and commands you need to encourage. Being these as soon as you feel he has settled in his new home. These are:

- ❖ Look.
- ❖ Sit.
- ❖ Stay.
- ❖ Come.
- ❖ Walking on the leash.
- ❖ Not to nip.

❖ Not to bark at everyone.

The last three rules are obvious, but the others are important too and will help you encourage good behavior.

Tips on Training the Puppy
Be Consistent

As the trainer, the first rule for you to learn is to be consistent. Don't get lazy on your part. Once you've begun teaching him your rules, you do need to keep it up.

Let's take an instance whereby you don't want Puppy on the couch other than at night time. This will confuse him because he can't comprehend that sometimes he can get up and other times he can't. To him, he's either allowed on the couch, or he isn't.

One way to get around this is to teach him that he can get up when you put his blanket there. If his blanket isn't on the couch, teach him to get down. This way you lay out the guidelines and perimeters for him. You must be consistent with this rule and don't let it lapse, or he will once again become confused. If you are not consistent and he gets it wrong, you only have yourself to blame.

Patience

To train a puppy, you will need to learn the art of patience because he'll be easily distracted. When you first teach him new commands, put him in a place where there are few distractions. This will be your training area. That way, he will have a better focus on what you are saying and doing.

Time

Do his initial training sessions in short bursts of 10-minutes, with at least 2 sessions a day. It doesn't seem long, but for a puppy, any time away from play is a long time. The treats should hold his attention for a short while. Once you've taught him a command or two, continue to use the training outside of the sessions. It might be a couple of weeks before he gets the hang of it, but keep it up; it's not forever.

Biting

Right from the onset, you must STOP him using his teeth for play. A puppy has 28 needle-sharp baby teeth. These will begin to fall out after 4 months, and then the chewing stage begins. First, though, you have to get through the baby-sharp stage. Teaching him at a young age will stand him in good stead for later in his life.

When puppies nip, it's usually because they are over excited. When this happens, have an alternative toy to offer him and take his attention away from your skin. He would have played at rough and tumble with his littermates. He would have used their teeth and learned that teeth can hurt, so he should already have an idea of this. Don't punish him though as this will only instill a fear response. With your free hand, pat his back or tickle his ear as he takes his new chew or toy from your other hand. It's important to make sure he feels safe and not fearful. Don't pat him for long though; you want his attention on his alternative biting object.

I stress once again, NEVER hit or slap him for his misbehavior. He may misread this sign and see a mild slap or push of your hand as your encouragement to continue play. A harder slap will only teach him to fear you, which can lead to so many other problems.

Not only will you need to teach the puppy, but you will also need to make your children aware of how to approach this problem. A very young child under 8 years of age will not comprehend all the rules, so always supervise them when together. After all, you want them to bond and enjoy one another's company. As an adult, that is your responsibility. That's why it is better to instill discipline in a gentle way right from day one.

Treats

We all know the best way to train a dog is with treats, but make sure they are small ones as he may get to eat quite a few of them. Check the ingredients to ensure they're also healthy ones. I'll talk about dog foods in a later chapter.

Look

1. To get your puppy's attention on the treat, teach him the command "look."

2. You might better kneel on the ground at his level if you are able to.
3. Hold the treat so he can see it.
4. When his eye has caught sight of the treat, delay giving him the reward for around 10 seconds and repeat the word "look."
5. Build this up by adding another 10 seconds until you reach a minute before he's getting his reward.

Sit

Now you know how to get his attention onto his treat, it's time to move on to the next command of "Sit."

1. Hold the treat, so he can see it and use your command of "look."
2. Once his attention is on his treat, move it above his ears.
3. You may find that when he follows the treat with his eyes, his bottom automatically sits down. If it does, then say the word "sit," before giving him the treat and "good boy" treatment.

4. If not, then gently push on his backend and say the command "Sit" firmly, until his bottom sits on the floor.
5. Give him his treat as he sits, and a little pat on the head as you say "Good boy." Don't make too much of a fuss. You want him to stay focused and repeat the action a few more times.
6. While you're training, try to use very few words. Stick to your specific command and praise words as much as you can.

Stay

Once your puppy can "sit" on command, move on to the command of "stay."

1. Have your puppy sit, but don't give the treat straight away. Once again, make him wait 10 seconds before his reward.
2. Add a further 20 seconds in stages, and say the word "stay" as you make him wait.
3. When you've achieved a whole minute, begin by taking a step backward at the point of 30 seconds. Stay there until the minute is up, all

the while repeating the word "stay." Give him his treat once this is achieved.

4. Add a visual training cue as you build up the distance. Stretch out your arm showing your puppy the palm of your raised hand while repeating the command "stay." He'll begin to associate that visual display with the command "stay."

5. Increase the steps backward, until he's waiting longer for his reward. All the time you are increasing the distance away from him and using the command word "stay."

Come

To finish off this set of commands is the word "come."

1. This is a command that can be incorporated into playtime in the backyard.
2. As you run around, use the command word "come" as he chases you.
3. Stop and tell him what a good boy he is with a little petting.

4. Once he's learned to "stay," begin using the command word "come" in the training sessions, rewarding him when he comes to you after "staying."

Congratulations!

You and your puppy now have a basic program of commands. He should now be able to sit, stay, and come when you use your command words. These will be very useful commands when he's running around in the park off the leash.

Leash

Before you head off out in public, he needs the training to walk on the leash. This can begin in your backyard if you have one. If not, then in the home, but it won't be easy in a confined space.

1. Use the command word "come." When he comes to you, put his harness or collar on along with his leash.
2. Begin by keeping the leash slack and walking in a straight line.

3. Whenever he tugs, change your walking direction, and say the "come" command.
4. The idea is to show him that he must go where you lead when he's on his leash.
5. As soon as possible, progress to a larger space, such as a dog walk outside the home all the while using these instructions.

Finally, we will look at how to stop the puppy from barking too much and in the wrong situation. Barking is his dog-talk, so he should be allowed to communicate in the right situations. When he's chasing his ball in the park or letting you know there is a stranger at the door. What you need to discourage is any incessant barking at anyone and anything. How then can you differentiate his barking noises?

Barking

❖ When he's playing and barking out of sheer delight, his yaps will be short and sharp. Of course, these yaps will develop into barking sounds, but they will still remain as short, sharp noises. These mean he's happy and having fun.

- ❖ If someone knocks at the door, his barking noise will become loud and in short bursts. They are distinctive bursts because they will have an urgency to them, making his barks closer together and faster. He's warning his pack that danger lurks close by. He needs reassurance that all's well. Don't reward him, or he'll continue to do it believing that's what you want. Nor should you yell at him because he'll think you're joining in the chorus of warning. Ignore him, with no reward. He'll soon become bored with his efforts of barking. It's as simple as that. Watch for his ears going back and his tail getting low, which are all signs of stress. .

A young puppy may run around excitedly to see who's at the door. If this is the case, then his tail should be wagging, and he'll pant as well as bark.

You, on the other hand, must remain calm and quiet. Use a command word to quieten him down, such as "quiet." Don't shout over his barking noises. Try and fit it in-between. If you have begun crate training, now is a good time to teach the puppy to go to his "crate" or "bed."

If you have an excitable puppy, it is going to take some endurance on your part, but remember to be consistent.

You must ignore a noisy dog. Only if he responds to the command word to quieten down can he have a reward. You could practice with family, friends, or even neighbors knocking on the door.

- ❖ When left alone, he will become bored. This can be when he starts to bark incessantly and annoy the neighbors. It is an obvious one to resolve. Either don't leave your puppy alone or try to make plans for someone to come and walk him. He has lots of energy to burn up if he's bored, and it needs to be used up before he'll settle down.

These are the basic house-training rules. If your puppy is not picking along as he matures, or you want him to be more obedient, then consider puppy training classes.

Chapter 8

Vaccinations and Puppy Academy

There may come a time when you either feel your training is unsuccessful, or you want his discipline to extend a little further. That's when you should consider puppy training classes. Not only will they be fun, but your puppy will get to socialize with other dogs too.

The puppy cannot mix with other dogs until he's at least started on his vaccinations. That's why it is better to initially start the training yourself rather than waiting. For some, that can be all the training your puppy needs. Others find professional training to be an additional help. At around 12 weeks old, he should be ready for his grand entrance into public areas. Some obedience classes are happy to take puppies once they've had their first set of vaccinations, as early as 8 weeks old. You would need to check with your local dog training centers.

Puppy's Vaccinations

Puppies need a little help to build up their immune system to certain diseases that could prove fatal. In the US, your puppy will need a regular course of inoculations:

6-8 weeks old

Distemper is a highly contagious and often fatal disease, with no cure. It might not kill immediately. A dog can suffer terrible reactions, such as fits and organ breakdown. Eventually, this disease attacks the nervous system. It is an airborne disease and often caught from certain wild animals.

Parainfluenza is a bacterial virus. It affects the airways and passes between dogs very quickly.

10-12 weeks old

This is a combined vaccination known as DHPP.

D = Distemper

H = Hepatitis (Adenovirus)

P = Parainfluenza

P = Parvovirus

Hepatitis is an infectious virus that can attack the liver. It spreads from other infected animals through body fluids, including feces. As there is no cure, all that can be done is to treat the symptoms. Adult dogs can recover, but it's unlikely that a young dog will get better.

Parvovirus can also be fatal for puppies, and again, there is no cure. It attacks the gut and rapidly dehydrates a dog. It is so potent it can kill within 48-72 hours of contraction.

12-24 weeks old

Rabies is an unpleasant and fatal disease. It spreads when a dog is bitten from an infected animal. Most states require this vaccination by law, but you can check with your local vet. Rabies leads to nasty symptoms with an unpleasant death. It is a disease that can be fatal for humans too.

14-16 weeks old
DHPP.

1-1.5 years old
Rabies and DHPP.

2 years old
DHPP.

Another bacterial infection that can be passed on from dogs to humans is Leptospirosis, which is also known as Lepto. It can be caught from mice and rats but is quite prevalent in the countryside. It is preventable with a vaccine. The problem in the past was that the vaccine proved controversial. Many owners complained of an adverse reaction to the injection. Their pets suffered symptoms such as vomiting, hives, and lethargy. More recently though, this vaccine has improved. It is now much safer than previous batches. Such incidents of adverse reactions have reduced considerably.

If you feel concerned about this vaccine for your puppy, then discuss it with your vet before making a decision. Lepto was initially for dogs who lived in rural areas and close to forests. Now, it is spreading among urban wildlife. Dogs that have Leptospirosis are contagious to other dogs as well as humans. The disease is often fatal causing liver or kidney failure.

Following this schedule, your puppy will need to continue with booster vaccinations as he matures. Most vets in the US do not advise yearly boosters anymore but to follow this schedule:

- ❖ Rabies - every 3 years after the first year, providing they have followed the first year schedule.
- ❖ DHPP - every 3 years after your puppy is 2 years old. Again, providing they have followed the first 2-year schedule.

This covers the core vaccinations that any responsible owner should ensure their dog receives. There are other optional vaccinations such as Lyme Disease and Kennel Cough. These can depend on where you live. Ask your vet about the optional vaccines and whether your puppy needs them.

Most pet owners are happy to have their pets vaccinated. It is good for the puppy and good for your wallet too. Treatment for some of these diseases can be very expensive. Your pet insurance will almost certainly demand that your puppy has his shots and boosters. Your pet insurance may not cover the costs of any vaccinations or boosters depending on which insurance package you have chosen.

Pet Insurance

The following information will give you a basic understanding of what your pet insurance can cover. It outlines the different types of policies that are available. The cost of cancer treatment alone can be in the range of $7000 or more, so you can see why pet insurance is essential.

- ❖ Accident-only coverage

It only covers accidents and will not cover any illnesses. It usually includes examinations and any treatment needed due to the accident, up to a certain cost. If your dog has an accident, the policy will cover other expenses such as:

- ~ Vet fees
- ~ Scans or X-rays
- ~ Small pay-out fee upon death. This is often limited by age, covering dogs only in their first 8 years.

There will be optional levels in the price of the package you choose:

❖ Excess Fees

This is the amount you must pay yourself which is usually the first $100 or so, dependent upon the agreement.

❖ Reimbursement Fees

You also choose your reimbursement percentage with most policies. This determines the percentage which the insurance company will pay back to you. The options are usually 70%, 80%, or 90%. The lower the reimbursement percentage, the lower will be your monthly subscription payment.

❖ Total Coverage

When choosing which policy is right for your puppy, you will need to decide the annual limit. This is the amount the insurance company will pay out in total for a year. These amounts can vary between insurance providers. The range is from $5000 to an unlimited amount. If you reach the limit, the insurance company will not reimburse any further veterinary treatment until the year is up.

Another factor to consider when taking out pet insurance is what is covered within the policy.

A comprehensive cover policy will cover conditions that include:

- ❖ Hereditary problems
- ❖ Accidents
- ❖ Illnesses
- ❖ Behavioral problems

It's also important to understand what is not covered:

- Pre-existing conditions. If your dog already suffers a condition when you start the policy or within the waiting time, it will not be covered by the insurance.
- Vaccination costs
- Or any other preventative measures, such as annual pet check-ups and any preventative screening, although some insurers do include these costs if you pay an extra premium.
- Cosmetic procedures, such as nail clipping, dentistry work, grooming, tail docking, or ear clipping; none of these are covered by your insurance.

How does pet insurance work?

Most insurance providers work on the basis that you pay the bill for the services first. Then you make a claim to your insurance company. If the services are covered, you will receive a refund of the costs. How much will be refunded will depend on your reimbursement percentage minus the excess fee.

Puppy School

Puppies learn better once they are socializing. The sooner you can attend a training class, the better. For instance, if your puppy is prone to nipping and won't stop despite your own training, then other dogs will teach him a lesson or two. When he left his litter, the natural rough and tumble with the other dogs stopped. At the same time so did his social training with other dogs. Once the puppy can mingle with his own kind again, he will quickly pick up on acceptable dog behavior. If he was to bite another dog, they would be quick to let him know that it is not acceptable. It's all about those natural social cues that we learn by socializing with our own kind.

Once you've decided to take your puppy to the classes, you should look into what makes an ideal puppy-training class.

- ❖ First and foremost, you must assess if the area that the dogs are to train in is clean. If it isn't, then turn away and leave. This can be a sign that the training school has low hygiene standards. The last thing you want for a young dog is the possibility of disease and illness.

- ❖ Has the Trainer asked to see your vaccination card? If they haven't, then turn away and leave. You must be confident that the other dogs attending are all checked for vaccinations before you send your puppy to the classes.

- ❖ Is the trainer approachable to humans too? You want to be able to ask questions, so it's no good if the training staff only like dogs. A good trainer knows that both dog and owner need training. They will encourage you to ask questions, so you can learn to help your dog throughout his life.

- ❖ Is there a calmness to the lessons or are they chaotic? The last thing you want is a trainer who doesn't have much control over the animals or people. Or even if they shouting a little too much, that is going to achieve nothing but fear in your puppy.

- ❖ Ask if you can visit when a lesson is in progress. Note if the dogs and owners are having fun. If they're not enjoying themselves, then it's doubtful that they're learning much.

- ❖ Make sure you are registered in a class that equals the level that your puppy is capable of. You may have already done some basic training, so there's no point starting right from the beginning. It's not a good idea to have beginners, intermediates, and advanced, all in the same training sessions.

- ❖ Class size is important too. Ideally, there shouldn't be more than 8-10 dogs with a single trainer.

- ❖ Avoid puppy classes that use water sprays or anything that makes a horrible noise for training purposes. However, a clicker is a good piece of training equipment. Training should be calm and organized, not cruel and scary for your puppy.

- ❖ Don't continue to attend a puppy class whereby the trainer makes fun or shames an owner that isn't doing it right. That can only mean one thing, and it isn't good that they are unsociable bullies.

- On a final note, don't compare your puppy's development to that of the others. He'll get there when he's ready, and you must accept this.

Equipment

There are a few basic rules expected of you as a dog owner:

- Take along your puppy's vaccination card in the first week. This shows the trainer he's up to date with his inoculations.
- Make sure your puppy is already comfortable wearing a collar or harness and lead. These will be a mainstay of the training ritual.
- Take along a bag of small soft treats for training purposes. These can be from chopped up dog treats to human foods such as cheese or meat pieces. It could be whatever you know your puppy likes best. The snacks need to be soft and easy to chew, so your puppy isn't spending ages trying to eat them. Vary the treats, so he doesn't get bored of them.

- ❖ You might prefer to take toys rather than treats, and that should be fine too, so long as the toys don't make noises or distract the other dogs in any way.
- ❖ Take a small bowl and a bottle of water. That way he can have a drink from his own bowl when he needs it.
- ❖ Take a blanket that's he is familiar with. When he's resting between training tasks, he has something familiar to lay down on.
- ❖ Don't wear your best clothes. It's more sensible to wear comfortable, old clothes as you might end up on the floor yourself.
- ❖ Don't forget the all-important poo bags; no one's going to clean up his mess but you.
- ❖ At around the 3rd week, you might need to take his grooming brush. This should be covered around then, in the training sessions.

Finding a Puppy Trainer

Once you've decided to have puppy professionally trained, it's time to find the local puppy-training classes.

- ❖ First port of call could be your vets. They should be knowledgeable about local training classes.
- ❖ You could also contact the American Kennel Club (A.K.C). They run a program called C.G.C (Canine Good Citizenship). They cover training sessions from "accepting strangers," to "walking through crowds." plus many other common situations and the basic commands we have already discussed. You can then move on to gain an array of training certificates, should you want your puppy to do well.
- ❖ Ask a local dog groomer.
- ❖ Ask other dog owners. There's nothing better than a recommendation if other dog owners assure you it's a worthwhile class.
- ❖ If all else fails, research them online at places such as The Association of Professional Dog Trainers https://apdt.com (APDT). You should also look up reviews from previous attendees to give you an idea of their services.
- ❖ When you find one, ask if you can visit for a session without your dog. This will give you an

idea of how good the class is, without the distraction of your puppy trying to join in.

❖ The cost of training classes can vary, ranging between $8-30. Much depends on whether you choose to be in a group or you prefer one-to-one training.

❖ Should you choose to send your puppy to obedience boarding kennels or training camp, this can vary between $1-2500. The disadvantage of sending your puppy to boarding kennels is that you won't be there to teach him. Plus, you might miss him, and he might miss you too. It's much better to be there for the initial training. Should you want to further his training, or his behavior becomes troublesome, this could be a quick solution to modifying problematic behavior.

Try a few different trainers in your area, if you can. Ask questions to help you decide which one will be best for your puppy and you:

❖ Check if they belong to a professional organization and if they hold the appropriate certificates. This will show you that they are an established and regulated school.

- ❖ Ask what methods they use in the basic training program? For example, do they use positive reinforcement, such as treats and praise? This is essential because training under duress is not acceptable.
- ❖ Do they hold other training sessions besides basic skills? Often, they offer many sessions, such as competitive dog sports or therapy training. If they do, it gives you an idea of how varied their training skills are.
- ❖ Find out what equipment is needed in the training sessions? This will give you an idea of what you should bring with you.
- ❖ How large are their classes? You don't want to join a class with more than eight to ten owners and their puppies, as this might get a little chaotic.

There's nothing wrong with joining puppy academy schools. They're a great way for both your puppy and you to socialize. You get to know how other people are managing, and your puppy gets to meet new friends. Socializing is an important part of growing up so that the puppy can enjoy the outdoors as he matures.

Chapter 9

Socializing

Dog Descendants

One sure way a puppy can learn the unwritten rules of socializing is to attend puppy academy. Socializing will be a part of the program, so it's an ideal place to start.

We all know that dogs are descendants from the grey wolf from thousands of years ago. Yet, studies have shown that they now have similar traits to humans when it comes to socializing. Whilst the wolf is a social creature, this is more in a territorial sense. Dogs though have developed social skills that their ancestors, the wolf, would never accept. Would a wolf even understand the facial features of a human, let alone react to them?

Dogs may not have had these social traits as a species originally. Selective breeding by humans has changed their natural behavior. Of all the traits strengthened in the breeding process, living harmoniously with humans has played an important role. The domesticated dog has evolved exactly how humans intended.

Up to the time of leaving their mother and litter siblings, a dog's instincts are to stay close to their dog family. A puppy is more responsive to learning new things up until the age of around 20 weeks. Studies have shown that if a puppy is not introduced to humans before 14 weeks of age, its acceptable social skills will be under-developed. This indicates how important social interaction with people is for a very young puppy. He's at his most receptive at such a young age. If he's left in the pack and only socializes out with other dogs, it will take much longer for him to integrate with humans. It can still be done, but the dog may have social problems. Just as it is harder for older humans to learn new skills, so too is the case for older dogs. Dogs though are resilient and very adaptable creatures. If you home an adult dog, it is still possible to re-train his behavior to suit your family needs.

The broader a puppy's early experiences are, the more balanced he will be as an adult dog. Puppyhood is the best time in his life to imprint those social skills upon him.

Instincts

The interesting aspect of socializing your puppy at a training school is that the other dogs there are not a part of his pack. This means he will learn how to cope with meeting dogs that don't "belong" to him. Out in the wild, wolves will fight with non-members in a territorial battle. Outsiders are rarely accepted into a wolf pack, though they may accept visits from extended family members.

There is no doubt that dogs are innate pack creatures. The difference is that they have learned, over thousands of years of development, to accept outsiders as friends. Teaching this to your puppy is essential, so he can fit in well with his environment.

The More the Merrier

A very young puppy hasn't quite grasped that he belongs to a pack. That would have developed into a territorial behavior in order to care for his pack. If he barks when the doorbell rings, that's his instincts kicking in. This is when you can change his behavior, so he overcomes those instinctual urges.

To overcome this instinctual urge, you can train a puppy to accept others who are not in his family. Make his training fun, so it challenges his mind. By meeting lots of new people and lots of new dogs, he will learn how exciting his new life is going to be. The busier his little life becomes, the more he will enjoy all the hustle and bustle around him. This is one of the advantages of puppy classes. There will be other puppies and owners who are all going through the same process.

If you could ask your puppy if he wants to play with other puppies, he's most likely to jump at the chance excitedly, the same as a human child would. Socializing at such a young age should be fun. They don't have any hang-ups yet, and if you teach them well, they will never get any social problems in the first place.

Integration of New Friends

If you already have pets, then your puppy is going to have some ready made friends as soon as he arrives at his new home. Whether this is in the form of another dog or even a cat, you must integrate them under supervision. The puppy will most likely be friendly towards his new friend, but you can't guarantee they will welcome him with the same enthusiasm.

Dogs will generally accept whatever other creatures already live with you, especially when introduced at such a young age. Needless to say that if you have a snake "loose about the hoose," your puppy is going to be very curious, so keep your eye on him.

Many dogs and cats live harmoniously together when introduced from a young age. They accept each other because they are so young. If you have an older cat, then that can be more problematic, especially if the cat is not used to dogs. The likelihood is that he will ignore the new puppy. If the puppy gets too close, then he's likely to hiss and give a warning swipe of paws. That should be enough to warn puppy off on a permanent basis.

If you have an older dog, then you will want them to get along together. You should be present as they are familiarizing with one another. Let your grown dog know that the new dog is not a replacement and continue to give him plenty of attention. The last thing you need is an older jealous dog on your hands. It should not be that way if you introduce them in the right manner.

It's unlikely your current dog will hurt the new puppy. He may show some aggressive behavior towards the newcomer, such as a deep growling noise if the puppy approaches. Don't punish your adult dog for growling. It is dog-talk and yet another way for the puppy to learn. The puppy doesn't know anything about rules at the moment, so you need to supervise him closely.

A grown dog will put up with quite a lot, but he must have an escape route. His growls should teach the puppy when he's had enough. If not, then the adult dog needs to be able to walk away. If there is no escape for the adult dog, that's when there is the potential for trouble. Make sure that your puppy can't go in all the places the adult dog goes.

When you first introduce them, keep your older dog on a leash. Make sure all his belongings are away, so the puppy doesn't get a hold of them. This may cause territorial jealousy. When they are together, praise the adult dog when he isn't growling, even to the point of giving him a treat. Don't over fuss the puppy in his presence. Reinforce a calm and peaceful setting for both of them. Keep an eye on the adult dog's body posture, because that should be your warning system. Are his ears back? Are his hackles raised on his back? Is he snarling and showing his teeth? These are all signs that he feels threatened.

It should only take around 3 weeks to get mutual acceptance between them. The older dog may never like the puppy but will learn to tolerate it with your help. They should have separate food bowls, separate beds, and even separate crates if you decide to crate train.

The advantage is that the puppy is about to get the best teacher ever, in the form of his new housemate. As they integrate more, the puppy will mimic his elder's behavior, so he becomes easier to train. Plus, the puppy will never be alone if there is another dog in the home. However, don't leave them alone until you are certain that your older dog has accepted the new arrival.

Chapter 10

How to Choose the Right Food

A puppy's weaning from their mother's milk onto solids usually begins at around 4 weeks of age. One of the obvious questions to ask your breeder is what solids puppy is eating. This doesn't mean that you must continue with the same food, but it's best to do so for the first week or so.

Balanced Goodness

When determining the diet for your new puppy, you must look to provide the right balance of calories, protein, fats, and vitamins. In the wild, dogs and wolves are mostly carnivores. Their diet consists of meat from prey or scavenged carcasses. Domesticated dogs have evolved since their wild ancestry, and so has their digestive system. Their food still needs to contain the right balance for a dog, such as:

Energy compounds

This includes carbohydrates that can come in the form of cereals and legumes. Carbohydrates should form only a small part of your dog's diet. Too much can lead to diabetes and obesity.

Proteins

For a dog, this is the most important element and should be at least 50% of your dog's diet. Proteins contain important amino acids that the body cannot produce. Dogs may naturally turn away foods that don't contain protein, using their natural survival instincts.

Fats

This is another important element of any dog's diet. Puppies need lots of fats and fatty acids for healthy skin and coat. Again, too much fat can lead to obesity in dogs.

Minerals

The top three are calcium for bones, magnesium for muscles and nerves, and phosphorus for energy and metabolism.

Puppies need more calories at this growing stage of their lives, and their calorie count will reduce as they get older. For instance, a puppy weighing around 10lbs will need around 900 calories a day, but when he's fully grown at around 33lb, he'll only need half that amount per day.

Overfeeding

One of the first things to ensure is that you are not overfeeding your puppy, most especially with the wrong type of foods. Doing that can only result in weight gain and lead to obesity and other related diseases. The last thing your dog needs is diabetes or a possible serious heart problem. That does not make for a happy life.

Puppies can also have voracious appetites, consuming anything in their path. Make sure he can't get into the trash-can because the smell of rubbish can be too much temptation.

Because puppies tend to overeat if left to their own devices, they can suffer from a distending stomach. This can lead to a serious condition known as Gastric Dilation-Volvulus (GDV). As his tummy dilates, it can twist at each end. This is known as "Torsion" and will build up with gas so that nothing can get out. It can be a life-threatening illness and will warrant immediate professional attention.

Symptoms of GDV:

- ❖ Extended hard stomach
- ❖ Belching up thick stringy mucus and saliva
- ❖ Unable to lay down because of stomach discomfort
- ❖ The puppy may pace around acting anxious, eventually collapsing.
- ❖ Fast panting leading on to shallow breathing as it worsens.

This is a rare but serious condition, and a dog can die within an hour of the torsion occurring. It can also become costly to treat if you don't have pet insurance. For the sake of your puppy's life, don't overfeed.

Feeding Schedule

A puppy needs a good feeding routine. That will enable him to digest his meals and also result in a good pattern for his toilet training. A good rule of thumb for a medium to large puppy is:

- ❖ 2-4 months old - 4 small meals a day with each meal around ½ cup size.
- ❖ 5-6 months old – 3 meals a day with each meal around ¾ cup size.
- ❖ From around 6-8 months old, spread those meals to 2 a day with each meal around 1 cup size. This should remain the same for its adult life.

If your dog is larger or smaller, then measure the meal size accordingly. For commercially produced pet food, check the labels. Manufacturers do provide instructions on meal sizes for the various-sized dogs.

Types of Food

This book is not about promoting brands, so we will avoid naming specific foods. Bear in mind that your puppy is doing lots of growing at such a young age. This requires a high intake of protein of around 20-30% of his diet for strong bones and muscles.

For the first year of your puppy's life, he will need soft, easily-digestible ingredients. If you buy commercially-tinned dog food, then a rice base with small chunks of meat is a good choice. Add a little kibble for something to chew on.

Homemade

Many pet owners do not like to use manufactured food to feed their dogs. Research indicates that many pet foods contain ingredients that can be harmful to for your dog. (Freeland 2012)

Besides the fact that homemade is best for pets and humans, you will still need to get the right balance. These meals should include ingredients such as:

Protein

White meats, such as chicken, turkey, duck, pork, lean beef, and fish, such as salmon. Whilst offal is okay for puppies, it is much richer and should not make up more than 15% of protein intake. Remove all bones from the meat or fish.

Fats

You can give the puppy cooked egg yolks and poultry skin. You can use oils, such as vegetable, olive, flaxseed, canola, and even soybean. When adding meat, use lean cuts, for example, beef fat content should be less than 10%.

Carbohydrates

This includes ingredients such as rice, potatoes, whole-wheat pasta, grains, and beans. Note rice and pasta should be the fiber-based brown variety.

Vegetables

These should be cooked and consist of ingredients such as green beans, peas, carrots, or butternut squash. They can be fresh or frozen.

Mineral and vitamin supplements for canines.

You can even crush up egg shells almost to a powder as a supplement for minerals such as calcium.

A puppy meal should be made up of:

- ❖ 20-40% vegetables.
- ❖ 40-80% protein.
- ❖ 20% carbs.
- ❖ 10% fat
- ❖ Plus vet-recommended vitamins and minerals.

You could make the meals up in bulk. All these ingredients can be frozen and then fully defrosted or refrigerated for up to 5 days. Use suitable containers like recycled glass bottles that human food comes in, such as jam jars, marmalade, and sauces. They all are good for storing puppy's home-cooked food in.

Here's a simple recipe to give you an idea of how easy it is to cook for your puppy.

Combine all the following ingredients into a large-lidded pan:

- ❖ 2.5lbs of ground meat (beef or turkey)
- ❖ Large can of rinsed kidney beans
- ❖ 1.5 cups brown rice
- ❖ 1.5 cups large chunks of butternut squash
- ❖ 1.5 cups of diced carrots
- ❖ ½ cup frozen peas
- ❖ 4 cups water
- ❖ Put the lid on the pan and bring contents to the boil. Simmer for an hour or until the rice and vegetables are soft.

You can even make homemade dog treats and biscuits. Such recipes only use common ingredients. Of course, don't forget to omit the sugar.

Other supplements and treats can be:

- ❖ Tinned tuna.
- ❖ Parsley (It helps to freshen breath).

❖ Yogurt (It provides probiotics that helps to balance their digestive system.)

Tinned Foods

Even if you don't want to produce your own dog food, this guide of ingredients should help you decide on the healthiest brands of manufactured dog foods. One very important word to look out for on tinned dog food is "AAFCO." This means the nutritional value has been met and recommended by the American Association of Feed Control Officials.

Kibble or Dry Foods

Puppies can have dried food, so long as there is plenty of water available. The problem with dried food is that it is highly calorific. One cup of dried food can be between 350-450 calories. One cup of tinned food would be around a hundred calories, so there's a lot of difference. If your puppy puts on too much weight, then you should look at reducing the amount of dried food you give him. Or add more fiber, such as cooked vegetables. Some people use a little bit of both when mixing wet with dry or tinned with kibble. If you want to give a mixture of dry and wet food, read the label instructions on how much to give of each, and halve both measurements. Puppy will still need water for that dried food.

Toxic Foods for Dogs

Raw Meats

It's not a good idea to feed a puppy raw meats. Their digestive and immune systems are not yet developed enough to cope with any pathogens. Such harmful microorganisms can lead to salmonella and other bacterial illnesses. In 2012, following their own study, the FDA (Food and Drugs Administration) advised not to give dogs raw meat. If you still prefer this option, then make sure you don't allow the dog to lick you. Nor should you let his paws contact your hands or face, in case they have touched the raw food. Should the food contain pathogens, these can be transferred to humans. By cooking his food, you will be lowering the risk of illness immensely.

Other foods to add to the NOT ALLOWED list, because they are TOXIC for dogs are:

- ❖ Chocolate
- ❖ Onions
- ❖ Garlic
- ❖ Avocado
- ❖ Macadamia Nuts
- ❖ Alcohol.

It's worth mentioning a website called Pet Diets.Com where trained animal nutritionists advise on specialist diets.

Chapter 11

GROOMING

Dog's Coat

Dog hairs are made up of similar compounds to fingernails, which is a protein compound called keratin. There are two basic types of dog coat: hair and fur.

Both hair and fur pass through the same growing stages, but hair goes through it slower.

- ❖ Stage 1: Anagen

This is the beginning stage when the root forms in the follicle gland. A root consists of cells and protein, fed by blood. Cells begin to grow, forming the hair/fur thread, which will continue to grow.

- ❖ Stage 2: Catagen

The next phase is a pause in the Anagen stage, and the hair/fur becomes bonded, so it no longer receives a blood supply for growth.

❖ Stage 3: Telogen

It is a stage when the hair/fur remains in the follicle gland, but in reality, it is now a dead strand of hair/fur.

❖ Stage 4: Exogen

The dead hair/fur strands now shed.

Hair Coat

These dogs are known as hypoallergenic breeds, such as poodles and Afghan hounds. Each hair strand is finer than a fur strand. A dog with hair has a single coat layer. The hair is usually longer or curlier than fur and grows slower. Hair is much slower to get through the four stages. Indeed, hair can stay live in the Anagen stage between 2-7 years.

Fur Coat

Fur has more follicles per inch of skin than hair, so it can be thicker. Most dogs have fur coats, which means there are two layers to the growth, with an undercoat and a topcoat. The undercoat is more of a fluffy soft downing and will keep them warm. The top layer will grow thicker and longer. However, there are some breeds that will only have one layer, which is the topcoat.

Shedding

Many dogs need their coats grooming only once or twice a month. There are some breeds that need very little maintenance of their coat. Short-haired dogs usually come under that heading. They may still shed their fur in the spring and autumn. This happens as they lose their winter coat and the weather turns warmer. When it turns colder, or in permanently cold climes, their coat becomes thicker. This is more prominent in dogs that are kept outdoors. Indoor-reared dogs may not be as affected by seasonal changes as they are warm all the time.

A dog with a single coat will shed much less than a dog with a double coat. The thick winter downing underneath needs to come away for warmer weather, and then grows back again later in the year. The topcoat, or single coat, will only shed once a year. Of course, all dogs will shed old hairs that are constantly replaced by new growth.

Puppy Coat

A puppy is born with a single coat. He sheds his puppy coat when he's 4-6 months old. That's when he will also grow his topcoat if he is a double-coated breed. For some breeds, it can be two or three years before their coats are fully matured. Until the coat is matured, they can often look a little bedraggled.

Pet grooming doesn't only mean looking after your puppy's coat. It involves other hygiene routines too. Many breeds need little maintenance, but there are some basic tasks you should do around once a month.

Bathing

- ❖ For puppies with longer fur, it's best to bathe them every 3 months. Though there are many breeds, such as Labradors, that never need a bath, that is unless they happen to roll in something that smells unappealing.

- If you want to bath your puppy more regularly, then be sure to use a mild soap, such as a baby shampoo. Watch out that your dog's natural oils in the skin are not getting too dry with the soap.
- Dogs don't care for slippery baths and may panic. If you have a shower without a slippery base, then use that instead.
- A dog's fur becomes quite heavy with the weight of water on it. It's best to keep rubbing it off his back when you can, so he doesn't fret too much.
- Avoid his head as much as possible and try not to get soap in his eyes, it will sting, and he may panic.

Grooming Services

You can bathe him yourself, or you can take your dog to a professional groomer. Specialists like this can help with many essential health and cosmetic needs, such as:

- Clipping and brushing the coat
- Cleaning teeth

- ❖ Clipping nails
- ❖ Cleaning ears and eyes
- ❖ Brushing out any tangles
- ❖ Killing fleas

You can find some pet groomers at pet salons. Ask about them at a pet store or even your local veterinary surgeon. As an alternative, you could use a mobile service that will come to your home to see to your dog's needs. Mobile groomers have the advantage of working with one customer at a time, and of course, your dog does not need to travel.

Before you choose a groomer, you should visit the salon to see how they handle their clients. Find out what soap products they use. This will give you an idea of whether you consider it will be a stressful experience for your dog.

If they ask you questions about your puppy's likes and fears, then you're in the right place. If they try to sell you their products or service packages, then leave. The difference is that those who ask about your pooch obviously care that they get it right. Ask if they have any qualifications. This is not a regulated industry, so if they've gone out of their way to gain certificates, it shows personal commitment, particularly so if they have a Master Grooming certificate. This is one of the more respected qualifications for pet groomers.

They should also welcome any questions you might have, and you really should ask questions. You need to know if they check vaccination updates. The last thing you want is cross-contamination of any of the diseases we discussed earlier. As with the breeder's home, you need to check the cleanliness of their salon. Don't be afraid to look at their towels too. If you feel really brave, you should ask how they launder them. You don't want your puppy picking up any skin infections.

If you go to a salon where dogs are wandering around in chaos, stay away. It should be a calm, controlled, and relaxed setting. Because they're using sharp instruments, such as nail clippers, unsupervised dogs could cause an accident.

Most groomers work on an appointment system and base their costs on how large your dog is. It may cost a little extra if your dog needs more attention, such as he doesn't like being groomed. A basic grooming package should cost between $30-$90. The average cost is around $50. There will be extra charges for extra services, such as nail clipping, teeth cleaning, or even a flea bath.

Chapter 12

Traveling

One reason for owning a dog is the amazing memories you will accumulate. Take him on vacations and long walks, and he will soon become a major part of your life. Whilst it is true that not all dogs like to travel, others love it. They learn that it means they're going somewhere fun, a place where they can run and bark and sniff out new smells.

You can train a puppy right from the start to accept travel as part of his life. Done correctly, there should be no reason why he can't join you on trips and vacations. It's much more fun for both of you than lodging him in boarding kennels and leaving him behind. Though, there may be times when Puppy can't travel with you for whatever reason. Later, we'll look at the options of where your puppy can go if this happens.

First, let's see how easy it is to train your puppy, so he will be comfortable when going out on road trips with you.

Laws are a little ambiguous, from state to state, on whether you should restrain your dog when traveling in a vehicle. There are proposals going through legislation to ban drivers from traveling with an unrestrained dog in the vehicle. At the moment, it's still unclear whether this will become illegal and thus a punishable offense.

Putting the legality aside, would you want your dog loose anyway? What if you were unfortunately involved in a vehicle accident? Not only could he get hurt if he gets propelled forward, but he could also hurt the people in front of him. This is a potential disaster. You owe it to your puppy and your passengers to consider all safety aspects before setting off on a journey.

Safety Travel for Dogs
Type of Vehicle

Make sure you have the right type of vehicle that can accommodate a dog. For example, a 2-seater is no good as dogs should not be allowed to sit in the front seat.

Whilst an airbag can save a human, it can be very problematic for a dog. The force of the airbag if it is deployed can seriously injure or even kill your dog. If he rides in front, he could end up under your feet or interfere with your driving of the vehicle. It may even be illegal in some countries, so check the local by-laws.

Placing a dog in an open pick-up truck is very dangerous. He could jump out and cause an accident with other drivers. This would be very traumatic, and he may lose his own life. This is an extremely irresponsible way to travel with a dog.

Securing your Dog

We have already established why a dog should not travel in the front seat, but nor do you want him loose in the back. Also, we have discussed the consequences of his body propelling forward should you need to do an emergency stop. This could be disastrous. How then can you ensure your puppy's safety when traveling?

- ❖ If you have a station wagon, then fitting a dog guard at the rear would keep the puppy securely away from all the seating. He can have his familiar bed with him, and he will be able to move around. Such guards can be bolted to the roof and floor, so it doesn't get displaced easily.

- ❖ With a station wagon or hatchback, you can situate the dog cage at the rear of the car. If you have a sedan type car, it should slot onto the back seat. For the smaller dogs, there are travel carry boxes that can also go on the rear seat. It would be better if the carry box is secured with a harness to the back seating area.

- ❖ Crate training proves useful when it comes to travel. If your car is large enough to take the crate, then this is the safest place for a puppy. A dog should be able to stand up and turn around when confined in a crate.

- ❖ Large dog hammocks are designed to fit across the back seat. They attach to the front and back seating headrests, resulting in a hammock type shape. It might be better to still use some type of dog harness if you can, as the dog can still propel forward in an accident. Such coverings help to keep the rear seats clean and free of dog hairs. These are quick and easy to fit on the rear seats and are removable when he's not traveling with you.

❖ Specialist harnesses or seat belts can be fitted that accommodate the shape of a dog. This will mean that he cannot move around very much, and he may not take to it very well, but he is as safe as he can be.

In all these methods, the puppy will still be able to see and hear you, so he knows you're still there.

Training Puppy to Travel

Just because puppy can't socialize publicly until he's started his vaccinations, it doesn't mean that you can't acclimatize him to traveling. Once you've decided on his method of staying safe in the car, begin by taking him out for short journeys. Start at 10 minutes around the block and increase to 20, then 30 minutes. Watch him closely, and see how he reacts to it. If he's sick, don't worry at this stage. It's caused by the new stimulus from the motion of the moving vehicle, which is an unusual experience for him. Chances are, given time, he'll adjust and grow out of it. If not, there are medications that you can use to reduce the risk of travel sickness. Don't use it immediately. Wait until he's around a year old before you give up on him getting used to traveling.

Here are a few tips for those practice sessions:

- ❖ Play soft music over the radio.
- ❖ Keep the car cool, use the air-con if you have to.
- ❖ Make sure he's got a familiar smelling blanket or bed to lay on.
- ❖ If he's sick, withhold food for at least a few hours before the journey. At least, then he'll have an empty stomach.
- ❖ Should he continue to be anxious and sick, then consider natural remedies first. Try adding certain scents to his blanket. Adaptil is a synthetic scent, but it replicates the smell of his mother's pheromones when he was weaning. Lavender is not only good for humans but also for dogs. You can buy a collar with Adaptil infused into it, so he can wear it for traveling. Or, you can use it as a spray, a tablet, or in a

diffuser, though you'll need a battery operated one. Adaptil does not harm humans in any way.

As the journey gets longer, make sure you carry a water bottle and dish for him so he can drink. Once the vet gives him the all-clear, drive to places where he'll get a good walk. The more he gets to travel, the sooner he'll accept it as a part of his life.

6 Travel Tips for Dogs

Now that he's a seasoned traveler and can go anywhere, there are certain rules you need to set in your mind. Call them common sense rules, but they are important for the wellbeing of your puppy.

1. Make sure he's microchipped and that the information is up to date. This is in case he jumps out of the car and runs off. Microchipping in the US is voluntary, that is unless you own a certain breed of dog that might be considered dangerous though it is highly recommended that you microchip your dog regardless of breed. It is inexpensive and

could ensure his safe return home if he goes missing.

2. Don't let him loose in a strange place, in case he wanders off. Even if he's microchipped, it will be a worrying and stressful experience.

3. Stop for breaks on long journeys. Not only will he need the toilet, but he needs fresh air and to stretch his legs, just as you will.

4. NEVER leave a dog alone in the car in hot or freezing weather. Have a look at these facts, and you'll soon understand why:

    ~ Outside temperature 70F.

    ~ Within 10 minutes, the temperature in the vehicle can reach 90F.

    ~ Within half an hour, it can potentially reach 105F.

Going by these figures, the temperature inside the car is always greater than the temperature outside. Considering this, imagine how hot it can get in the car if it reaches 105F outside.

Dogs quickly become ill with heatstroke when confined in a very warm vehicle. This can result in dehydration and even death. Please DO NOT take that risk with your dog's life. Even with the windows open, it will not stop this from happening. He is in a metal box. Your pet cannot sweat; all he can do is pant to try and cool off. This is useless when he is surrounded by such hot air. If his body temperature increases by only 2 degrees, it can be fatal.

Whatever it is you need to do out of the car, it is not worth his life! Take him with you.

5. If you are traveling overseas with your dog, then check what procedures you need to follow. There are International Certificates that dogs need for certain countries. Research your destination's local laws and get it right. If you don't, you may end up facing a hefty fine and paying for your puppy to be quarantined for many months.

6. On the topic of vacations, now you have a puppy, be sure to include him in future holidays. There are plenty of pet-friendly hotels in most countries. Okay, you may not be given a luxury room because of your dog, but his

company is worth far more than classy furnishings.

Leaving Puppy Behind

Your puppy cannot go with you all the time, so you need to think about how you want him to be cared for if this happens. Here are a few options to consider:

Boarding Kennels

There'll be lots of other dogs at the boarding kennels. Usually, they each have their own separate kennel but can still be within proximity to other dogs. Visit the kennels without your puppy much the same as you would a puppy school.

- ❖ It should not have an overpowering smell of urine or feces. The kennels ought to be thoroughly cleaned out on a regular basis. Do they hire enough staff for this to be done? Either walk away or ask further questions, but bad smells mean bacteria is lurking.

- ❖ The dogs shouldn't be barking all the time. Sure, there will be some noise, but it should at a minimum if the dogs are not stressed.
- ❖ If they don't ask to check your vaccination papers, then don't use them. All dogs going into boarding kennels should be up to date with their shots because they will be socializing together when exercised.
- ❖ Ask what their daily routine will be, so you can see if it suits the needs of your puppy. If it doesn't suit your puppy, there is no harm in asking if they can accommodate certain things your puppy is used to. If they refuse, then it's up to you whether you think your puppy can manage, or you can look elsewhere. Often, these kennels have lots of dogs to care for and cannot accommodate individual needs.
- ❖ Although this can be expensive, it is the cheapest method of making sure they are cared for in your absence. If you have more than one pet, you can often get discounts on multiple bookings.

Private Sitter

This means hiring someone who cares for dogs professionally that is unless you happen to have a loving relative or neighbor. There are two types of private sitters:

- ❖ A dog sitter comes into your home at set times to feed, clean, and walk your puppy. They don't do the housework while they're there, I'm afraid. What a shame!
- ❖ Puppy stays in the dog sitter's home. This is the most expensive. It does mean that your puppy is in close contact with people all the time you are away. It's usually people who are animal lovers that do this. A good dog sitter will allow you in their home for a pre-visit, and so you can have answers to all your questions.

Whichever type you use, do check their reviews. These should be from past customers who have used their services. They can be vital in helping you to make the right decision.

Chapter 13

THE DREADED WORMS AND FLEAS

Internal Parasites

Dogs easily pick up the worm's eggs in poop or grass. The minuscule eggs might stick to their paws, or they may lick them up. They can also be transferred from infected dogs or wildlife. If the mother has worms, she will transfer them to her pups. The other common way to catch worms is through fleas.

If your puppy becomes infected, you should go to the veterinary surgery. He will need a course of injections. The first set is to kill the adult worms, then another set 2 weeks later to kill the larvae as they come out of the eggs. This can continue until your puppy gets the all clear.

Humans can also become infected, so you should ALWAYS wash hands after cleaning up dog poop. For this reason, do not allow a dog to lick your hands or face. Young children are prone to catching them when playing in areas where dogs have pooped.

Hookworms

- ❖ Small, thin worms under an inch in length.
- ❖ Attach to the intestinal walls with tiny hooked teeth.
- ❖ Feed on blood and soft tissue.

Symptoms

- ❖ Loss of appetite and possible weight loss.
- ❖ Diarrhea.
- ❖ Blood in stools.
- ❖ Itchy toes or skin.
- ❖ Anemic pale gums.
- ❖ Coughing as the worms migrate into the lungs.

Roundworms

These are the most common in puppies and can be treated after a puppy turns 3 weeks.

- ❖ White or brown and resemble spaghetti, up to a few inches in length.
- ❖ Feed off digested food in the intestines.

Symptoms

- ❖ An Unexpected loss of weight.
- ❖ Diarrhea and vomiting.
- ❖ Excess lethargy.
- ❖ Potbelly that doesn't go away.
- ❖ Dullness in the coat.
- ❖ Worms may appear in poop if infested for a long period.

Tapeworms

- ❖ Flat and segmented. Each segment is about the size of a piece of rice.
- ❖ Adults can reach up to a length of 28 inches.
- ❖ Live in the smaller intestine.
- ❖ Segments that contain eggs become detached and are expelled through the dog's poop. These segments re-infect another dog.

Treat flea infestations immediately as these are main transference of roundworms.

Whipworms

- Around ¼ inch in length.
- Attach to the lining of large intestinal walls.
- Thick body with a thin tail-end, hence the shape of a whip.
- Digested by licking an infected area of the eggs or through the mother's milk.

Symptoms

- Weight loss.
- Diarrhea.
- Blood in stools.
- Excess lethargy

To determine if your puppy's illness is due to a worm infestation, a trip to the veterinary surgery is best. Tests will be undertaken on your dog's feces. That means you need to take a sample along with you.

Heart-worms

They are prevalent in the US and caught through mosquito bites. They are difficult to control infection, so preventative treatment is the most effective. Heart-worm treatment also prevents the other worms we have discussed in this section. This is easy to administer and can be done at home. It is far better to take this non-invasive precaution than risk your puppy becoming ill unnecessarily.

Fleas

You cannot stop fleas from jumping onto your puppy. If your puppy has been treated, the fleas will die. Fleas can jump between animals, i.e., from cats to dogs, and they can lay dormant without a host for a few days at a time. In the cold, though not freezing, the eggs can lay dormant for months. Anything with hair is prone to fleas and ticks, though different animals suffer from differing types. They have some purpose in the ecosystem of life, so they are here to stay.

Here are some chilling facts:

- ❖ A female flea can lay up to 500 eggs in her lifetime.
- ❖ That single female flea's offspring will also lay eggs that can equal a thousand eggs within 3 weeks.
- ❖ Arm yourself with the knowledge that a flea, at any stage of its life, will die in temperatures below 37F. Although this can take up to 2 weeks, so if the temperature rises, they will not die.

How then can you help keep puppy flea free?

If your puppy does catch fleas, it can be a long process to remove them all from his coat. Then you must treat the rest of your home, including the outdoor areas where he plays. Often, it can involve chemicals that are not very pleasant. Once again, prevention is best.

Home Remedy for Infestation of Fleas

Here's a home remedy if your puppy has picked up fleas and you don't want to use a commercial product:

Puppy's Treatment

- ❖ Give a good old-fashioned bath with a mild non-sulfate soap. Create suds to rid those troublesome fleas from the coat. Rinse your dog in diluted apple cider vinegar. Fleas hate the smell, so they won't be jumping back on the puppy any time soon. This particular vinegar helps the coat to gain back the correct pH balance after the soapy suds bath.
- ❖ Follow this with a good inspection of the coat. Have a flea comb at hand to get out any remaining adult fleas, dead or alive, and any eggs you might find.

Indoors Treatment

- ❖ Wash all dog bedding, and put out in the sun to dry or in a hot dryer for 15 minutes, if the materials allow. The heat will kill any remaining fleas or eggs.
- ❖ Cover your floors in an equal mixture of salt and baking soda, which kills the eggs. Leave it on for 24 hours. After that time, you can

vacuum everywhere, particularly in dark places where fleas like to hide. Immediately empty the vacuum bag as any live fleas will lay dormant waiting to escape. Meanwhile, they may also lay eggs.

- ❖ Keep vacuuming every other day for the first week. Vacuuming helps to move eggs in a carpet or on upholstery, so if you have pets do vacuum often.

Outdoors Treatment

- ❖ Mow down any long grass making sure there is no poop anywhere.
- ❖ If possible, expose shady areas to sunlight, as that could be where the fleas are hiding.
- ❖ You can spread "Nematodes" around the garden. These are tiny living worms that eat parasites at a voracious rate. They'll also remove slugs from your garden too. Don't worry; they don't harm pets or humans.

Preventative Treatment Against Fleas

Some commercial products can be used as early as 4-weeks old or when your puppy weighs at least 2-lbs.

These products range from flea shampoos to collars and sprays and even come in the form of a tablet. You can stop tick or flea infestations all year round, with the right products. Speak to your vet to discuss the right kind of preventative medicine for your puppy. If this is too costly, then do some research to find a method that is affordable.

It is important to understand these basic major causes of illnesses that a puppy is prone to picking up. The key cure for worms and fleas is preventative treatment. That way, you can avoid any of the associated illnesses that can come with worms and fleas.

Chapter 14

POSSIBLE HEALTH CARE PROBLEMS

I would like to recount a funny story that happened to my family. We had welcomed our new Staffordshire Bull Terrier pup into our home. Finally, after her immunizations, we got to take her out on her first walk. Within 10 minutes of returning home, she began running around the room in frantic circles, followed by little distressing puppy yelps. Was it some sort of seizure? Had she eaten a poisonous plant on her walk? As this incident occurred on a Sunday, our vet was not open. We contacted them urgently to get out the on-call vet; they opened the surgery for us. Our hearts were in our mouths as we watched the vet assess our very distressed little puppy. What was he going to find? Would we lose her before we had even got to know her? It was a very stressful situation - for a short while.

Well, it turned out that it wasn't some horrible blood clot on her brain. She wasn't having any seizures or any of the other horrible scenarios that played out in our heads. The cause of the mystery illness was that she had been stung on the sensitive soft pads of her paws. The culprit was a weed called nettles. They're quite harmless but can give a nasty little sting.

Even now, 15 years later, we still smile at the lovely little memory. All that erratic behavior was down to a tiny nettle sting. Of course, she didn't understand what was numbing her feet; she only knew they hurt. The whole family was so relieved that it was nothing serious, other than a hefty vet bill. All was well, and she lived on to enjoy old age.

The moral of this story is not to panic if you think your pooch is poorly. Dogs often suffer a little diarrhea from time to time. It could be that they ate something disgusting on their walk that you missed. Or, maybe they've got overexcited at a houseful of visitors they're not used to. There are many reasons a dog might be under the weather, but you should never ignore any of the signs.

Common Illness
Diarrhea

If your puppy's poop is runny, keep your eye on him for a couple of days. Watch for the following:

How is his appetite? If it's not too good, give him much smaller meals but more often for a couple of days. If he's still not eating after this, try some home-cooked dog meals such as the meals we mention in our food section. Ask yourself if he simply doesn't like what you're feeding him. Believe it or not, dogs can be picky eaters, especially the smaller breeds.

Sickness

If he's vomiting, feed him something easy to digest, such as scrambled eggs or rice with small pieces of soft chicken. Only give him his main meal, missing out the other meals. Try a tiny snack from your hand, of a piece of dry food if you have some in.

With either diarrhea or sickness or both, you should make sure the puppy is drinking plenty of water throughout the day. Diarrhea and vomiting can quickly cause dehydration.

If the symptoms persist for more than a day or two, you will need to take his illness to the next level, particularly if your puppy is shivering and whimpering. The trembling can be due to lack of glucose. They will then become lethargic with a high or low temperature. Try rubbing some sugar water or any sweet syrup you have, on their gums to help raise their blood sugars. If you're concerned, then take your puppy to the vet.

Temperature

- ❖ Normal body temperature for a dog is 101-102.5F.
- ❖ Anything above 104F or below 99F will need immediate attention.

Call your vet and explain, requesting a quick appointment. Dogs don't sweat but instead pant to cool themselves down. It might be worthwhile having a thermometer on hand. The best way to take a dog's temperature is by inserting the thermometer gently into their rectum. The nose will likely be dry and warm, and the skin on his belly will be warmer than normal. Remember though, a dog's temperature is a few degrees higher than a human, so he may feel warm to the touch, but it could still be normal. Also, if a dog's ears are cold, it is a good indicator that their body is cold. Don't over worry though because there are not many blood vessels to the ears, so he's not ill, just a little cold.

Common Diseases in Puppies

Because their immune system is not at its full potential, there are some potentially-fatal diseases that puppies can be prone to catching.

Parvovirus

This is a viral infection that can be caught if the puppy does not have his vaccinations. It is spread when dogs lick poop or infected animals; it's not surprising that sickness and diarrhea are the first symptoms. Look for blood in the poop, and it will smell exceptionally foul. For dogs that go untreated, up to 90% have had fatal results within a few weeks of infection. Remember, this disease is completely preventable with the correct vaccination.

Distemper

It is another viral infection that can be prevented through vaccination. It's an airborne disease caught by the animal breathing it in. Puppies can die within a week of transmission; it is that deadly. First symptoms would be a high temperature. This might be accompanied by "cold-like" signs, such as runny nose or eyes. Later, symptoms will include diarrhea and vomiting as the virus moves to the gut. From there, it goes on to infect the nervous system and the brain.

Kennel Cough

It is so named because it can spread like wildfire and infect every dog in a boarding kennel. It is a nasty respiratory disease caught from an infected dog. Again, your puppy may show signs of a cold with a runny nose or eyes and sneezing. In some cases, it can then develop into pneumonia. If the symptoms persist for more than around 3 days, go to your vet for treatment. There are preventative vaccinations and medication, but they do not provide 100% protection.

Skin Irritation

We have discussed parasites that can cause worms. They can also cause skin irritation in puppies, such as Demodectic mange which is a form of scabies. All dogs already have the parasite known as Demodex, but for most of the time, it lays dormant. Because puppies under 18 months of age have a weaker immune system, the parasite can cause problems if they catch it. If your puppy presents bald patches on the face, chest, or front legs, this may be the cause. Fortunately, it rarely poses any further risk than that, and it will go away.

If there are any secondary effects, such as soreness from itching, then you can bathe the puppy in an antibiotic shampoo. These are available from your veterinary surgery and will help to ease inflammation. There is also an oral medication or an injection called Ivermectin. There are other medications. If your puppy cannot have these, your vet will advise you better on this treatment.

The cause in the first place was a weakened immune system. If your puppy is unlucky to develop puppy mange, do reconsider his health. Is his food nutritious? Is he infected with fleas or worms? Either of these can that make his immune system weak. The stronger he is, the less likely he will be to develop such conditions.

Other Health Issues
Neutering

Unless you intend on breeding your dog, you should have him/her neutered at a young age. It helps to reduce aggression in male dogs. That alone is an excellent reason to neuter. It will also stop him from wandering off to look for females.

If you don't have your female puppy spayed, then she can come into season (estrus cycle), between 4 months to 2 years of age, depending on breed. That means that when you exercise your bitch, any male dogs that have not been neutered will attempt to mount her. They may even enter your backyard to get to her, as she gives off a strong smelling hormone that attracts male dogs. The estrus cycle will last anything from 1 1/2 to 2 weeks, again dependent on the breed. You may also find mucus stains on your furniture and floors. Expect this to happen around every 6 months, even more often for the smaller breeds. She will also be keen to get to the males, so it won't be easy to control her. If she is successful and manages to get out, then she will mate.

Do you want to be responsible for bringing puppies into a world where there are so many homeless dogs? Be responsible, and it will benefit the whole family and your dog. The best time to neuter is between 6-9-months because they are hitting puberty around this age. One sign that male dogs have reached puberty is that their testicles will descend and the will lift their legs to urinate.

Neutered dogs can tend to be a little overweight in later life. That can be controlled though, with care and attention. One more negative aspect is that it's unlikely the operation will be covered by your insurance. Allow for this in your budget when determining the costs of raising a puppy.

Self-Inflicted

This can range from eating foreign objects to having accidents in rivers and fields as they run around on their walks. They can fracture bones, break teeth, or even get stuck somewhere. It makes quite an amazing tale what vets have found in puppy tummies. From glass marble to stones from the backyard, they will eat anything and everything. All you can do is watch them closely, and attempt to train them not to pick up objects with their mouths. Good luck with that one!

Old Age

It seems only right to discuss old age and the expected life-span of your puppy before we complete our guide. It is inevitable that you will outlive your loving companion. Throughout his life, it will be a privilege to have him by your side.

As with the typical health issues in his puppy years, you can also expect health issues in his senior years. You have been there with him every step of the way. Losing a lifelong companion is an emotional bombshell, but this is, hopefully, in many years' time to come.

One of the first signs of old age can be when he becomes snappy around younger dogs. It could be arthritis setting in, and as younger dogs jump around energetically and knock him, he won't be happy.

Tooth decay and gum disease are also typical in an older dog. It's not as if he's been able to clean his teeth every day, as we humans do. Unless you've kept up with his oral health, as his immune system slows down, this can be one of the first places to suffer decay.

Older dogs can suffer similar symptoms as humans such as loss of hearing, unable to see as well, and loss of other basic senses.

They may put on weight as you slow down their exercise routine, so you should also adjust their diet. They will not need as much protein but nor do they need many carbs.

Incontinence can occur, particularly if he's on medication or suffers kidney problems, which is quite common in senior dogs. Treat this condition the same you did when he was a puppy, never chastise him for such accidents.

As his fur turns grey and he lacks the enthusiasm he had in his youth, it's time to slow things down in his life. He still needs his daily exercise, but instead of him running off to covering a wide range of ground, he'll prefer to stick by your side on his walks.

Life Span

Dogs live on average between 10-13-years. That doesn't mean to say your puppy won't live longer than this. Some dogs can reach 15-years old, or in rare cases even older. Smaller dogs tend to live longer than larger breeds due to fewer health problems. The Great Danes and other huge breeds of the dog world, may only live up to 8-years old.

If you want an idea of how dog years are calculated in comparison to human years, here's how the American Kennel Club break it down:

- ❖ By the time your puppy is 1-year old, he is the equivalent of a 15-year old teenager.
- ❖ At 2-years old, his aging has slowed down, and you will add only 9-years into his second year. He is now the equal of a 24-year old.

- ❖ From thereon, each year is equivalent to 5 human years.

Smaller breeds are considered senior dogs from around 7-years old, and larger breeds around 5-years old. These are the milestone years when you will begin to notice changes in your dog's behavior, that are age-related.

All these facts are useful to know because your puppy will be with you for its entire life. He relies on you to care for him, so you need to be aware of the changing stages. They will happen gradually and not suddenly. It's not something to worry about, but any responsible dog owner needs to understand the lifespan of his dog.

Conclusion

It may seem that when you read about all the factual information of rearing a puppy, there is much to consider. By researching the topic, you are taking a responsible approach, and that is all your puppy can ask of you. You are showing that you hope to give a puppy the best quality of life because you care. Don't let all that information put you off, because it does not amount to anything that you cannot handle.

Owning a dog can be the most rewarding of experiences. Well, actually, you don't own him, you are simply his carer. He will compensate you more than you could ever imagine. Your dog will remain loyal to you for its entire life, always by your side.

This guide will help you understand some of the problems that may, or may not, arise. We have set out solutions to show you that whatever problems occur, there are ways of dealing with them.

We have covered:

- ❖ Assessing your finances to ensure your puppy is not an extra burden on your budget. This will prepare you for the ongoing costs of keeping a dog, such as insurance, boarding, and food.
- ❖ The necessity of adequate pet insurance for any unexpected events.
- ❖ Basic commands that you can teach at home or how you can find professional dog behavior training sessions at a puppy school.
- ❖ How your puppy should travel in a car and alternative boarding options if you can't take him with you.

From the basic vaccinations that could save your puppy's life to being informed about the benefits of neutering your pet, we have discussed many of the common illnesses and how to deal with them.

These are some of the issues we encourage you to consider, even before you bring your puppy home. You have brought a puppy into your life because you want to, so it seems only right that you do it properly. That way, he is not only going to be a happy puppy, but he will also mature into a happy adult dog and live with you until a ripe, old age.

www.ingramcontent.com/pod-product-compliance
Lightning Source LLC
Chambersburg PA
CBHW031112080526
44587CB00011B/939